Kindness
Boomerang

Kindness Boomerang

How to Save the World
(*and Yourself*)
Through 365 Daily Acts

Orly Wahba

FLATIRON
BOOKS
NEW YORK

www.flatironbooks.com

The Library of Congress Cataloging-in-Publication Data
is available upon request.

ISBN 978-1-250-06693-0 (trade paperback)
ISBN 978-1-250-06694-7 (e-book)

Our books may be purchased in bulk for promotional,
educational, or business use. Please contact your local
bookseller or the Macmillan Corporate and Premium Sales
Department at 1-800-221-7945, extension 5442, or by e-mail
at MacmillanSpecialMarkets@macmillan.com.

First Edition: January 2017

10 9 8 7 6 5 4 3 2 1

This book is in memory of my captain, my grandpa. He may have lived a simple life, but his legacy is far from simple. He didn't only speak words of kindness; he did much more than that. He lived them and by so doing inspired myself and every family member to live kindness through and through. To you, grampsi, our captain, thank you for paving the path for us to follow and equipping us with the tools and confidence to pave our very own path in the spirit of kindness, love, tolerance, and compassion. Here's to the road not yet traveled, the path not yet taken, the change awaiting to be discovered. And here's to all those out there courageous enough to take the journey with me one step at a time.

Introduction

When kindness is shared it grows. And every bit of kindness we put out into the world comes back in some way. That's the kindness boomerang. I wrote this book of 365 daily acts, reflections, inspirational quotes, and stories to help remind myself and others of ways to spread kindness to those around us. Each day of the year has an entry, but you can jump around or ignore the dates altogether. I focus on twelve different themes of kindness, each denoted by a symbol, and I encourage you to read the ones you find most meaningful and share the ones that may not apply directly to your own life. If you are no longer in school, share acts of kindness in the school with a young person in your life, or if you're still in school, share acts of kindness in the workplace with others you know in the professional world. I welcome you to make this book a part of your daily routine or simply pick it up from time to time. Kindness has no limits.

I was a middle-school teacher for seven years in Brooklyn, New York, before leaving to found my nonprofit Life Vest Inside in 2011, with a mission to make kindness a global trend. During my time teaching, I had the unfortunate task of helping my students cope with a death in our community. In January of 2007, I boarded a plane to set out on a family vacation. During an airport stopover, I checked my voice mails, and received the tragic news that a young girl from my community had passed away. As a teacher, I had already encountered grief in my classroom—just three years prior, my students had lost a classmate, and right before winter vacation they opened up to me about it for the very first time, asking questions that aren't exactly easy to answer. "Why do bad things happen to good people?" "Why did she die at such a young age?" I had just started to get through to them and now they would be faced with the shock and pain of yet another tragic death. Naturally, my first reaction was panic: How would I help my seventh-grade students make sense of yet another tragic loss? How do you find order in such a chaotic world? How do you stay afloat when so many of life's events seem to pull you downward?

Moments after I listened to the voice mail, I boarded the second plane for my connecting flight. As I sat dazed and disheartened, I looked to my left and a small sign caught my eye: "LIFE VEST INSIDE." My eyes fixated on those three small words, I smiled and felt an instant comfort. A life vest has the ability to stay afloat regardless of how much one may push down upon it. Our life vest, our ability to overcome our hardships, to make it through, comes from "inside." Through the kindness we bestow on others and through the kindness others bestow upon us—we help keep each other afloat in the stormy seas of life. We can't prevent life's obstacles, mishaps, and curveballs from coming our way, but what we can do, what we have the power to do, is to throw someone a life vest, a lifeline of kindness. Perhaps they may still be surrounded by the rough waters of life, but that vest is the difference between life and death; giving them the hope that they can pull through.

Kindness changes lives, it helps us rise after we fall—and the moment I saw the words "LIFE VEST INSIDE" on that plane I made a conscious commitment to spread that message to the world. I would never have imagined back then that those three small words would in fact become something I live by.

One of the first things I did as CEO of Life Vest Inside was make the video *Kindness Boomerang*, which shows how one act of kindness inspires another and another, and finally comes full circle. I was lucky enough to get the wonderful song "One Day" by Matisyahu, one of my favorites, to play in the background. This video has now been viewed over twenty million times.

I've been the recipient of so much kindness in my life that it's inspired me to live more kindly toward myself and those around me. It's a ripple effect that begins with one simple act. I hope this book begins a trend of kindness in your own life.

Kindness
Boomerang

January 1st

★

Act: Create a list of goals for the day, the week, the year. You have an immense amount of potential and can achieve more than you can imagine. First step is reminding yourself of that!

Quote: "Your past is not your future. You have the power to make new decisions for your life starting today." ~Deb Sofield

Reflection: The greatest mistake we can make is allowing the guilt of what we haven't yet achieved consume us. Working off of negativity will never get you very far. Instead of looking at the gap between where you are and where you want to be, stop for a moment and look behind you at how far you've come and the small goals you've achieved. Use that momentum to propel you forward so that you can reach your next goal, your next achievement. Here's a tip: It's better to create smaller, more attainable goals than one larger-than-life goal. Break things down into their steps and climb the ladder one rung at a time.

January 2nd

Act: Make today "Judgment Free" in words, and, most important, in thought. Let's work on altering the way we think about others. The way we judge others is often the way the world will judge us.

Quote: "By judging others we blind ourselves to our own evil and to the grace which others are just as entitled to as we are." ~Dietrich Bonhoeffer

Reflection: What is judgment but fear of admitting our flaws and insecurities in our beliefs? Simple introspection and acknowledgment that we are all human and, at times, make errors in judgment equips us with the ability and know-how to see the other side of the coin.

January 3rd

Act: Get into the habit of saying "yes!" to the small favors and requests your family members make of you.

Quote: "Never underestimate the difference you can make in the lives of others. Step forward, reach out, and help." ~Pablo

Make-a-Choice Reflection

Scenario #1:

Your friend: "Can you pick me up from the train?"

Your response: "Sure! Let me know when you're a stop away and I'll be ready for you."

Scenario #2:

Your sister: "Can you pick me up from the train?"

Your response: "Can't you just walk? It's freezing outside?"

Sound familiar?

Family members are like friends you keep forever. Why is it so much harder to do kindness with those closest to us? We know in our hearts they will be there regardless of our mistakes or if we disappoint them. Isn't that a reason to celebrate our family? A reason to say yes when given an opportunity to give back to them knowing that they will have our back through thick and thin? Make it a point to give a second thought to the way you respond to your family today. Once you see the impact, you won't have it any other way.

January 4th

♥

Act: Memories can re-create special moments. Reach out to an old friend and reminisce about a time you both shared together.

Quote: "The best and most beautiful things in the world cannot be seen or even touched—they must be felt with the heart." ~Helen Keller

Reflection: Why do we fear reaching out? Perhaps the thing we fear most is that we've been forgotten, that the memories we so fondly recall are only significant to us. Remember this: If those moments meant a great deal to you, the likelihood is that they meant a great deal to the person you shared them with. Allow yourself to be vulnerable.

Life gets busy on all ends, so be mindful not to place blame or point fingers as to why you haven't kept in touch. Feelings of anger, hurt, and resentment will prevent you from reconnecting with those people in your life that you've drifted from.

So, get those photo albums out and take a stroll down memory lane until the memories become so strong that they appear before your very eyes. When you open your heart you may be surprised to find a piece of yourself that you have lost sight of.

January 5th

Act: Be polite on the phone today!

Quote: "Life is short but there is always time for courtesy."
~Ralph Waldo Emerson

Reflection: From telemarketers, to your spouse or friend, to employees, your distant aunt, or your mom calling for the twentieth time to see what you'd like for dinner, be mindful of how your words impact the day of another. You may not be able to chat for long, but communication is never about the words, it's about the tone, the inflections of the voice, and the way in which those words are said. It will take the same amount of time to utter them in kindness or frustration, but one will leave a person feeling uplifted while the other may change the trajectory of their entire day.

January 6th

Act: Our environment needs a little loving. Start becoming mindful of recycling. It may take you an extra moment to find a garbage can or recycling bin, but think of the impact. Let's take a step toward a cleaner world for us all.

Quote: "Love the world as you love yourself." ~Lao Tzu

Reflection: Ever wonder why the cleanest places stay clean, while the extra dirty places seem to get dirtier? Our actions or lack of action is often a reflection of our surroundings and environment. Here's something to consider: Are you more or less likely to throw trash on the ground in a city whose streets are immaculate as opposed to one whose streets are decorated in an assortment of waste? The cleaner the space, the more likely we are to want to keep it that way. The problem arises in a space where recycling is out of the norm. Let's break the habit and do our part, recognizing that if each and every person made a small effort, the job would be done. Instead of speaking words of kindness for the environment, let's live it and be a model for others to follow.

January 7th

🍎

Act: Before you leave class, thank your teacher for a great lesson. Two small words with a big impact.

Quote: "Kind words can be short and easy to speak but their echoes are truly endless." ~Mother Teresa

Reflection: As a teacher, there are times when I question myself. Did I have an impact? Did I even make the slightest change? Did I leave a mark? It's quite curious and equally wonderful that a simple "thank you" infuses a teacher with the endurance to overcome the tough days and wake up the very next day ready to open her heart and give of herself wholeheartedly.

January 8th

🌐

Act: Donate old books to the library. It may very well become someone else's all-time favorite.

Quote: "Let us remember: One book, one pen, one child, and one teacher can change the world." ~Malala Yousafzai

Reflection: Rarely in life do you find an object that retains its ability to continuously impact regardless of how many times it has been used. A book may first appear as a collection of pages filled with information, knowledge, and stories yet to be told. But in between the lines lie endless opportunities, possibilities, and dreams for the unsuspecting reader still discovering who they are as they contemplate the next chapter waiting to be written in their very own book of life. A good book can inspire one person to change their world, thereby changing the world as a whole.

Act: Take a moment to offer words of gratitude to a bus or taxi driver and let them know how much you appreciate their service.

Quote: "A compliment is something like a kiss through a veil." ~Victor Hugo

Reflection: "I see you." Three simple words we all crave to feel. They don't need to be uttered or shouted from the rooftops. They simply need to be felt in a smile or a warm greeting. There's beauty in the moment when two sets of eyes connect and an energy is magically transferred. To see beyond the labels, beyond the titles, beyond the collars. And suddenly what's left is the person: their heart, their soul, and their essence.

Act: Find yourself waiting in a line today? Break the ice and engage in a few minutes of conversation with others. Not only will the time go by faster, you may come out of it with a new friend.

Quote: "Courage is the power to let go of the familiar."
~Raymond Lindquist

Reflection: I will always recall one short interaction I had with a complete stranger while waiting in line in a crowded restaurant. Long lines, big crowds, and wait times often cause instant irritation but when I think of this particular situation, I can't help but smile. We could've complained like so many others. Instead we made light of the situation, shared some words back and forth, and transformed the mood and agitation of all those waiting around.

The way I see it, each person we come in contact with has something they are meant to offer us and something we are meant to offer them. It may not be measurable in money, connections, success, or the like. You may gain a new friend but you're more likely to gain a new perspective. We all have something unique to give, to teach, to inspire, to instill. It's not always communicated through words, but it still exists. Shed the labels, shed the fear, shed the insecurity, and take a chance.

Act: Know someone looking for a job? Lend a hand and assist them with their job search or résumé writing. Your guidance could help them land an opportunity of a lifetime.

Quote: "Do not let what you cannot do interfere with what you can do." ~John Wooden

Reflection: Procrastination, fear, and uncertainty are what I like to call the enemies of progress, preventing us from pursuing our dreams and achieving the goals we set for ourselves. Often all we need is a little push. A friend of mine, Jacq, needed this push when she decided that the time had come for her to leave her job. Working as an executive assistant was never meant to be her endgame, but like so many of us she became comfortable. She was ready to take the leap and begin the daunting task of rewriting her résumé, but, naturally, the "enemies of progress" reared their ugly heads. Jacq wasn't fighting them alone, though. We jumped on a call and together took the first step in starting a new chapter of her life. She didn't know where it would lead, and neither did I, but I knew I couldn't be happier to receive the opportunity to get her one step closer to her goal.

January 12th

❦

Act: Know someone who is struggling with the ups and downs of life? Gift them an inspirational book that has uplifted you and given you hope in times of need.

Quote: "We must accept finite disappointment, but never lose infinite hope." ~Martin Luther King, Jr.

Reflection: It can be found in a beautiful sunset, the smell of the grass on a spring day, the laughter of a child, an inspiring story, a hug, or a smile. For me hope was found in the words of a favorite book. Reflecting on all of the advice I had given throughout the course of my years, I came to realize that dispensing advice is far simpler than heeding it. Sometimes we need to take a step back to have the courage and strength to take the next steps forward. We may be unaware of where they will go, but we can be content in knowing that at least we have the hope they will go somewhere.

January 13th

⭐

Act: Dream big! It's the dreamers of the world that save us all—so never stop dreaming.

Quote: "Don't tell me the sky's the limit when there are footprints on the moon." ~Paul Brandt

Reflection: There will inevitably be days when you don't feel you can conquer the world, when perhaps you feel as though the world has conquered you. But remember, it is precisely in those moments of weakness when you are given an opportunity to find a great strength within yourself that you never knew you had. Have courage and be strong—because you're worth it and no one can take that from you if you don't let them.

This goes out to all those who need a reminder that someone out there is betting on them, even if they've stopped betting on themselves for the time being. Remember, hope is never lost.

January 14th

Act: Be confident. Be brave. Use your voice! Stick up for someone even if they aren't around.

Quote: "True character is what you say and do when no one is looking." ~John Wooden

Reflection: Choices don't simply dictate the lives we lead, they impact the lives of those who choose to follow us. It's one thing to choose the right path when others have treaded that path before you; it's another thing to create your own. So when you're faced with a choice, choose to inspire, choose to empower, choose to stand for those who have lost the will to stand for themselves. Who you are isn't determined by the amount of people watching you, but rather by your choices when no one is there to judge. Doing the right thing is not always easy, but then again the things in life that are worthwhile never are.

January 15th

🏠

Act: Have a family member that is starting out on a new venture or perhaps contemplating pursuing their dream? Encourage them to push full speed ahead. Don't allow your fears to dissuade them from taking the leap.

Quote: "Everyone needs a house to live in, but a supportive family is what builds a home." ~Anthony Liccione

Reflection: When I decided to leave my teaching job after seven amazing years to start a nonprofit with the sole mission of spreading kindness in the world, everyone thought I was crazy. I didn't have the funding or the experience, but I did have the dream. I had the passion and the conviction to answer the question of "why," knowing full well that if my heart was in the right place the "how" would find its way to me. Often discouraging words are simply a reflection of one person's inability to envision their dream being actualized. If a person lacks the belief that they can achieve their dream, how can they possibly presume to think anyone else can believe it? A few encouraging and supportive words have the power to make what was once impossible possible. You may think someone is just a "dreamer" with the inability to actualize their dream, but a little support from your end can tip the scales in their favor.

Act: Love someone for who they are. By doing so you may realize that they are already what you need.

Quote: "Being happy doesn't mean everything is perfect, it means you've decided to look past the imperfections." ~Gerard Way

Reflection: It's once we see a person for who they are that we can begin falling in love with the qualities that make them unique. No one is perfect. It was never meant to be that way. The challenge is seeing beyond the imperfections and uncovering the hidden gem that lies within them. I've found that the more we learn to see the hidden gems within ourselves, in spite of our tendency for self-criticism, the easier it becomes to spot them in others.

✸

Act: Take a genuine interest in a friend's culture and background. What a great way to find the beauty within our differences.

Quote: "Be curious, not judgmental." ~Walt Whitman

Reflection: Our differences are reasons to celebrate. A picture painted with various shades of the same color is far less appealing than combining many colors and their various tints, hues, and shades, each color giving the painting greater depth, meaning, and beauty.

January 18th

❦

Act: Share the acts of kindness, courage, and bravery that you have committed in an effort to protect our planet, the animals, and the people that afford it meaning.

Quote: "A single act of kindness throws out roots in all directions." ~Amelia Earhart

Reflection: Purity of heart mixed with genuine humility ensures that when we share our wins we are doing so for the right reasons. In today's world of digital media, one person can easily turn into thousands—i.e., one person has the power, through a single post, to impact millions. Now, more than ever, we need not question the validity and life span of our efforts. Every positive action has the potential to inspire, motivate, and empower someone that you may have never met and may never meet to make a change, give back, and contribute something positive to the world. Someone out there is waiting for the inspiration that you alone can provide. The only question that's left to ask is what are you waiting for?

January 19th

🍎

Act: Hold the door for someone. Simple enough, and you may just make someone's day.

Quote: "Remember there's no such thing as a small act of kindness. Every act creates a ripple with no logical end." ~Scott Adams

Reflection: After giving one of my former students an Act of Kindness card that read, "hold the door open for someone," I received a phone call the very next day with loads and loads of excitement coming through the other end. "You won't believe what happened after you gave me the card yesterday!" I listened attentively guessing what his next words would be. "Everywhere I turned there was a door that someone needed to be opened! It was crazy!" I smiled, chuckled, and said, "Those doors were there yesterday and the day before—but it's only now that your awareness is heightened that you're really seeing them!" You'd be surprised by the endless kindness possibilities out there. It's all about increased awareness. Let's start seeing the world through the lens of kindness.

January 20th

Act: Offer to help a neighbor or friend shovel snow or do yard work. Roll up your sleeves and show the world what you've got.

Quote: "No man is an island, entire of itself; every man is a piece of the continent." ~John Donne

Reflection: Living in New York, winters can be tough. When the snow sets in, it can be hard to get around. As a student at Brooklyn College, I used to throw a shovel in the back of my good old Jeep Wrangler and drive around campus after a snow storm hit, eyes peeled for someone in need. I was on a mission. After one particularly bad storm, I found a middle-aged man doing the very best he could to get his car out of the snow. When he looked up, seeing a girl shoveling away took him a bit off guard. "Miss? You don't have to do that," he said. "I want to. I insist," I said. He could tell from the look in my eyes that I wasn't backing down any time soon. We exchanged smiles, continued shoveling, and the conversation that followed generated enough warmth to take the bite out of the cold winter air.

January 21st

Act: Bring back a souvenir for one of your friends or family members the next time you head out on a vacation, road trip, or any kind of adventure.

Quote: "It is when you give of yourself that you truly give." ~Kahlil Gibran

Reflection: Small gifts purchased with loads of love can outshine the most expensive present. It's simply noticing that it's not about the gift at all. It's about the gesture, the thought, and the acknowledgment of the person you care about.

January 22nd

Act: Give an extra hand and help someone remove his or her luggage from the conveyor belt at the airport.

Quote: "Every action in our lives touches on some chord that will vibrate in eternity." ~Edwin Hubbell Chapin

Reflection: As a kid, I always had a fascination with the conveyor belt at the airport; the excitement of spotting your luggage and rushing over to pull it off. My two older brothers usually beat me to it. As an adult often traveling alone, the opportunity was now mine. I loved helping people I didn't know lift their luggage from the conveyor belt. I would spot an older couple or a parent flying solo with a handful of kids. It was a small gesture but it made me feel awesome every time I did it.

After getting into a pretty bad accident and injuring my wrist, lifting was no longer a simple matter. A stranger saw the struggle I was having, ran over, and lifted the suitcase off the conveyor belt for me. But he didn't stop there. Moments later he brought a cart over. Naturally we began to chat and hearing his story inspired me further. "After my surgery it was so hard to get around. I remember appreciating the small things people did for me and since then I do my best to find moments when I can pay it forward even in a small way," he said. Who knew that the extra helping hand I had given excitedly to others would find its way back to me?

January 23rd

Act: Introduce yourself to the "newbie" at work. Make them feel welcomed and share something about yourself.

Quote: "Getting money is not all a man's business: to cultivate kindness is a valuable part of the business of life." ~Samuel Johnson

Reflection: Warm words spoken from the heart can instantly melt away feelings of trepidation and intimidation.

At twenty-one years old, I walked into my first day of teaching middle school. My heart was pounding and endless questions filled my mind. "Would I be a good teacher? Would I make an impact? Will they like me?"

I took a deep breath and entered the school with the same fear and apprehension of a first grader on their very first day. I may not have been a full-fledged newbie, having been a student in the school only eight years prior, but it most certainly felt that way.

"You're gonna do great! They would be crazy not to fall in love with you right away, bubala," Mrs. Orlow, my former sixth-grade teacher, reassured me. Mrs. Orlow had a way with people; it's what made her the amazing teacher she was.

I may have still been nervous and anxious as I walked into my very first class, but there was a calm, a stillness, and the reassurance that someone believed that I had what it takes. I had yet to know that that very day would be the beginning of a seven-year journey responsible for changing my life in the most extraordinary way.

January 24th

🦋

Act: Don't jump to conclusions. Give someone the benefit of the doubt. We all know what it feels like to be misunderstood.

Quote: "Minds are like parachutes—they only function when open." ~Thomas Dewar

Reflection: The gifts we give to others sometimes have a way of coming back to us at the moments we need them most. Pointing fingers is easy; pausing to understand the perspective of another takes a great deal of courage.

How different would the world be if we all strived to have eyes that see the best in people, a mind that forgets the bad, and a soul that never loses hope that a person can become a better version of themselves? Knowing all too well that we all make mistakes in our own way, why place judgment on someone simply because they make mistakes differently than you do?

Strength is believing in someone when they've given up the fight of ever proving that they are worth believing in. Remember, anyone can find the dirt on someone; be the one to find the gold.

January 25th

✦

Act: Make the time to head to your favorite spot and let every one of your senses take its fill.

Quote: "Worrying does·not empty tomorrow of its troubles, it empties today of its strength." ~Corrie ten Boom

Reflection: Whether it's the boardwalk, a park, your favorite bookstore, or anywhere in between, if you allow it to your happy place can have the power to restore calm in your life.

Day after day we run about from one task to the next, fighting to keep up. When we do find ourselves with a solitary moment, we tend to store it up hoping to one day cash in on those few seconds of time. But as the days pass those moments escape. Seize the moments that are before you instead of planning for future moments that get lost in the abyss of time.

After one particularly hard month, I finally decided to make time to head to my happy place: the beach. With every step on the golden sand I felt life and energy returning to parts of my soul I had unconsciously neglected. I took a deep breath and while my to-do list remained as long as it had been from the moment I got there, I was suddenly filled with a renewed sense of purpose. I felt recharged and the to-do list transformed into a road map. I took my next steps with the confidence to see my journey through until the very end.

January 26th

■

Act: Commit to reading a book about values or ethics.

Quote: "Character is simply habit long enough continued."
~Plutarch

Reflection: Slow down. Perfecting your character isn't a marathon, a race, or a competition. It can only be won in stride with daily motivation. The key: Don't read the book all at once. Remember, you aren't simply reading, you're absorbing. Set aside five minutes every day to open yourself up, allowing the words to penetrate your mind and, most important, your heart. The real work begins after you put the book away and head out into the real world. With a little focus you'll find that opportunities to implement the words and teachings will be more apparent than ever. Nope—it's not magic. Those opportunities were always there. You are simply becoming more aware of them.

Act: Enjoy the gift of storytelling. Call or spend time with your grandparents or an elderly relative or friend. You'd be surprised by how much you can learn from the experiences they've been through.

Quote: "And in the end, it's not the years in your life that count. It's the life in your years." ~Abraham Lincoln

Reflection: "We're on our way to Nana's house, Nana's house, Nana's house so early in the morning." I remember singing these words as I bounced up and down with excitement in the car to head out on the five-minute drive from my house to Sunday brunch by my grandparents' apartment. As a child I didn't recognize just how lucky I was to be able to frequent my grandparents' apartment with such ease. It felt as though this opportunity would last forever, and it was years later, during my car rides to the hospital to visit my grandpa, that I wished I had made the five-minute journey to their apartment more frequently. Seize the precious moments and make the most of them. It simply requires us to pause within the chaos and frenzy of life. There is a great deal of wisdom and foresight in the words and the hearts of the elderly; soak it all in and you'll soon see that you too will bestow those pearls of wisdom on another.

January 28th

♥

Act: Have faith in yourself. That's right; sometimes the hardest kindness to do is for yourself.

Quote: "Faith is taking the first step even when you don't see the whole staircase." ~Martin Luther King, Jr.

Reflection: Faith and belief in your capabilities aren't things someone can give you. They must be developed, nurtured, and cultivated by no one else but you! Believing in yourself when times are good is a given. The question is whether you can withstand the urge to give up when the road ahead isn't so clear, and it seems as though you are in the midst of a storm with no sign of refuge. Every person must and should go through their very own period of hardship and discovery bringing them to call on an inner strength they wouldn't have found if not pushed to the limits. You may not have achieved the long list of accomplishments you thought you would have already crossed off, but never stop believing in your ability to reach your goal. Practice a bit of understanding with yourself and hold close to your heart the words of Walter D. Wintle, "Success begins with a fellow's will. It's all in a state of mind."

January 29th

◉

Act: Be considerate. Become mindful of waiting for a person to finish speaking before interrupting to add your thoughts. So simple, but often overlooked.

Quote: "If I had it to do again, I'd ask more questions and interrupt fewer answers." ~Robert Brault

Reflection: Everyone has a story, an experience worth sharing, or a lesson they can teach. Whether we learn from it and grow from it is up to us.

Often the want and desire for our voices to be heard overshadows the voices of others. It prevents us from engaging in perhaps the most instrumental lesson of all. The lesson that is inherent in the simple act of listening.

A powerful leader, like a conductor, need not say a word for his message to be communicated. His sole function is to listen and guide others through opposing viewpoints, away from their own agendas and objectives, to hear one another amidst the noise in an effort to add to the progress and development of the whole. To turn the mere sounds into music, the mere ideas into action, the mere voices into echoes of change.

A little self-restraint and patience can be hard to practice, but invaluable once mastered.

January 30th

Act: Give our air supply a breather. Be mindful of how you use or misuse paper.

Quote: "Infuse your life with action. Don't wait for it to happen. Make it happen." ~Bradley Whitford

Reflection: Mindfulness is simply the ability to observe, to notice, and to be aware. What you decide to do with that knowledge is where the impact lays. Mindfulness is the first step to thoughtfulness and the first step on the road to change. Clean air may seem like a given to those unaffected by air pollution, but let's remember that there is only one planet earth and we have collectively been tasked with ensuring its survival. While our actions or inactions may not be reflected back at us instantaneously, negative outcomes are never the effect of choices we make in the moment but rather a series of continuous choices to turn an eye and make it someone else's battle.

January 31st

🍎

Act: Make a handmade birthday card for someone in your class and have everyone sign it!

Quote: "I value the friend who for me finds time on his calendar, but I cherish the friend who for me does not consult his calendar." ~Robert Brault

Reflection: Celebrating people in our lives is a privilege. A birthday card does so much more than just acknowledge the date of someone's birth; it magically gives us, as the giver, an opportunity to reflect on the friendship we have, the lessons we've learned, the memories we've shared, and the gratitude we hold. That in itself is something to truly celebrate.

While I was never much of a fan of my own birthday, there was no task I loved more than choosing a birthday card for someone else. I would spend hours breezing through the aisles of Hallmark, searching for the perfect words, the perfect card, and perfect emotional force to embed into each word. What would I want and hope for someone to share with me on my birthday? I knew I had an opportune moment to brighten someone's day and I wanted to take full advantage.

Act: Do something special for a neighbor to let them know how much you value their friendship.

Quote: "The everyday kindness of the back roads more than makes up for the acts of greed in the headlines." ~Charles Kuralt

Reflection: My close friend Jeff has always been known as the caretaker. He loves being there for people and they love relying on him. But even a caretaker can get ill from time to time, and as a giver it's never easy to ask for help.

After being ill for over two days, with no food in his system, immense pain in his body, and barely the will to move, Jeff weakly knocked on his neighbor Ivan's door. Ivan may not have been extraordinary in conventional ways, but accomplishments aren't the sole measure of a man's value. What truly separates one person from the next is his or her willingness to step up and be there for another with no motive or intention of reward.

Without hesitation, Ivan drove Jeff to the hospital, and went the extra mile by picking up his prescription and liquids to help nurse him back to health. Ivan could've stopped there, but what made him extraordinary was his determination to ensure that Jeff would fully recover. He called Jeff every hour on the hour to check in. He may have said it was his neighborly duty, but Jeff called him his angel.

February 2nd

Act: Be the designated driver. Keep your friends safe by offering them a ride after a long night out. Drunk driving isn't cool and your act can save lives.

Quote: "Become the kind of leader people would follow voluntarily, even if you have no title or position." ~Brian Tracy

Reflection: Leadership is the vision and conviction to do what's right in spite of the myriad of people begging and pleading for you to do what's wrong. Being a leader is no simple task. It's filled with doubt and uncertainty. A leader often finds himself standing alone trying to see the clarity in a somewhat foggy and convoluted picture. But remember that it's easier to go along with something when everyone else does. It's a far greater challenge to hear beyond the noise and pick up on the subtle sounds that can only be heard when listening to the silences and empty spaces within that noise.

February 3rd

Act: Have a knack for music? Put your talents to good use. Arrange to stop by a nursing home and play piano for the residents. Music, just like kindness, uplifts the soul!

Quote: "Where words fail, music speaks." ~Hans Christian Andersen

Reflection: Music has the amazing power to uplift, strengthen, and inspire.

Community service trips were part of the curriculum at the middle school where I taught. The students loved the trips, but with their excitement came a sense of hesitation and fear.

"What do I say?" "What do I ask?" "What if they don't want to talk to me?" The kids piled into the school bus and with every block came more questions as we headed off to visit a local nursing home.

During that school year, I had directed the seventh-grade play production of *High School Musical* and it was common practice for students to break into song just about anywhere at school. It was no different that day. Within a few minutes, the bus filled with song and suddenly an idea formulated.

When the residents of the nursing home took their seats in the social hall they were greeted by a room full of smiling kids and the beautiful sound of their voices. It did more than uplift, strengthen, and inspire the residents of the nursing home, it wiped away the fear of the students and filled them with a sense of purpose.

February 4th

✿✿

Act: Is your office short on the basic manners like saying hello, please, and thank you? Give a genuine heartfelt greeting to your coworkers as they head in and out of work.

Quote: "Be kind, for everyone you meet is fighting a hard battle." ~Philo

Reflection: A friend of mine, Robert, made it a point to make every single person who stepped into his office feel welcomed and loved. When I first met Robert I told him some of the obstacles I was facing with the organization. Like myself, Robert founded a nonprofit he was extremely passionate about and faced daily struggles to keep it afloat. The most immediate and impending obstacle facing me that day was finding a space to work. Up until that point I had been working from my parents' home, but in a month that luxury would come to an end. Robert didn't hesitate for a moment. "Done!" he said and offered me the opportunity to work from his office space. Turns out the donated space was only the tip of the iceberg. The warmth, generosity, and kindness from this man have been unparalleled. But the thing I look forward to most is the amazing greeting he so wholeheartedly bestows as I walk in each morning and leave each night. "Orly's here! Now my day can begin!"

He calls himself the president of my fan club, but I must say that I am most certainly his biggest fan. For teaching me the value of a simple, heartfelt hello—I thank you, Sir Robert.

February 5th

❦

Act: Donate blood or make an appointment to donate blood today. You might save a life.

Quote: "The true meaning of life is to plant trees under whose shade you do not expect to sit." ~Nelson Henderson

Reflection: I was always petrified of needles. My mom often recalls, with horror, the scene I would cause in the doctor's office during our annual shot day. I'd make a dash for the bathroom and lock the door.

After starting Life Vest Inside I would post an act of kindness on the Facebook page each day; a simple action we can all do to bring about some form of change. A suggestion came through. Why not encourage the Life Vest Inside family to donate blood? The fear and embarrassment crept back in; how could I possibly encourage others to do something that I have never done and was so fearful of? As fate would have it, a big community blood drive was being held that week. This was my chance to face my fear and inspire others while doing so. I hesitantly posted about my fears and admitted that this was my first time donating blood. To my surprise, messages of encouragement poured in from people sharing the same concerns.

My name was called. It was time. I took one look at my phone, which had been blowing up with messages from others pledging to donate as well, and suddenly the fear disappeared. I'll never forget that day and the excitement knowing that with each passing second I wasn't simply donating blood, I was empowering others to do the same.

February 6th

✦

Act: Start an exercise routine. Whether it's three times a week, once a week, or as simple as five minutes a day. Taking care of YOU allows you to be your very best.

Quote: "What you get by achieving your goals is not as important as what you become by achieving your goals." ~Zig Ziglar

Reflection: While it's true that the journey of a thousand miles begins with the first step, it is precisely that first step that can often be the hardest to take. The biggest mistake we can make is giving up on our goal simply because we couldn't follow through on it to the letter of the law. Life doesn't have to be all or nothing. It's amazing how just doing something will pave the path to achieving so much more. Missed your scheduled exercise time? Don't fret. Resolve to get yourself to the gym tomorrow. But be careful not to fall into the trap of procrastination. Exercising your body is vital to the well-being of your mind. So head out for that run and see how much more focused you'll find yourself when you sit back down and continue plugging away at work.

February 7th

Act: Whether you believe in God, the Universe, or anything in between, take a moment and say a few words of prayer for someone in need of a bit of healing.

Quote: "Dare to reach out your hand into the darkness, to pull another hand into the light." ~Norman B. Rice

Reflection: Our thoughts become things. Repeat that to yourself time and time again and you will simply catch but a glimpse of your awesome power to impact change in the world.

When you find yourself lost in the worries of your life, take a step back and send positive thoughts and prayers to someone else out there. It makes no difference whether it's someone you perceive to be more or less well off than you are. When we see beyond ourselves, and our own wants and needs, hopes and aspirations, we are more likely to create ties with others who will do the very same for us in our time of need.

February 8th

🏠

Act: Who's up for a pillow fight? Spend some quality time with your sibling(s) or childhood friends. They will help you reconnect to a part of yourself you may have lost sight of over time.

Quote: "Family is not an important thing, it's everything." ~Michael J. Fox

Reflection: When I was a kid, all week I would patiently and anxiously wait for Saturdays. Counting down the days to when my siblings Joey, Robby, and I would escape to the basement and begin constructing the most awesome fort you could imagine. Each week brought a new secret mission, a new pretend world, but the same good old fun. As the younger sister, I'd most likely have to do all the annoying tasks of setting up the fort while getting picked on, but honestly there was no place I would have rather been. For a few hours on Saturday everything would disappear and I got to be with my two heroes, my brothers.

As we get older, escaping into an alternate world becomes less of a reality. Consorting with schedules, Google calendars, and the intense list of responsibilities can be daunting and often dissuade you from finding the time. Pick up the phone, clear some time in the schedule, and you'll see that the time spent with people from your childhood can magically transport you to that unforgettable fort of dreams. You'll surprisingly find that the short amount of time you've carved away for those people nourishes a piece of your soul you've neglected.

February 9th

♥

Act: Play cupid today and introduce two friends who may hit it off. Be mindful that you aren't setting them up for the wrong reasons.

Quote: "The meeting of two personalities is like the contact of two chemical substances: If there is any reaction, both are transformed." ~Carl Jung

Reflection: Traveling down the road of life singlehandedly is most certainly possible, but the joy and happiness created when one person finds their counterpoint in another is immeasurable. You can have a hand in the happiness of another and all it takes is keeping your eyes, mind, heart, and soul opened to see how connections can be made. We've been conditioned to believe that for one person to be at the top someone else must be at the bottom. This is simply the brainchild of insecurity. The more happiness we bring and infuse into the world, the more happiness is reflected back at us. I never would have thought that such a simple phone call would lead to such a beautiful marriage. When my friend Adam called me late one night asking if there was someone I might know of to set him up with, I initially couldn't think of anyone. Suddenly one girl's name popped into my mind. Annie, one of my former students. Suddenly it was as clear as day. What a perfect match! I quickly made the necessary calls and after a few conversations with both of them—a match was made. Dancing at their wedding was a joy I'll never forget.

February 10th

⚫

Act: Go out of your way to attend a wedding you might not have attended.

Quote: "Life is not about waiting for the storm to pass. It's about learning how to dance in the rain." ~Vivian Greene

Reflection: If someone took the time to invite you, take the time to stop by. Do away with the endless excuses and justifications you tell yourself. We all fall into that trap. Break the trend. An unlikely experience may be waiting for you.

I was exhausted, emotionally drained, feeling far from attractive, and hoping for an excuse not to get out of my pajamas and go to a friend's wedding. Suddenly, a perfect excuse came up. The snow began to fall in what became one of the worst snowstorms I had ever seen. As the snow got higher and higher and the cars driving outside became fewer and farther between, I began to feel a pit in my stomach as I turned my mind to the bride and groom and the likely empty reception that would await them that evening. A text message went out letting people know the wedding was still a go. It no longer felt like an obligation, it was a privilege. To share in the joy of a bride and groom, to sing and dance and remind them that they are loved. As I walked into the hall I was touched to see that so many made the extra effort, filling the hall with more people than I had ever seen at an ordinary wedding.

February 11th

◈

Act: Plant a tree! Whether you physically plant the seed or make a donation, you can rest assured knowing that you have added more beauty and life to the world.

Quote: "Wisdom begins in wonder." ~Socrates

Reflection: Nature speaks to us in more ways than one, empowering us simply by living its message.

I've always found myself fascinated by trees. They make me wonder. Give me hope. Even with the force of gravity weighing down upon them they grow, strengthen, and build. In spite of the pressure to not rise above, to not reach, the tree continues to overcome.

A tree is uninterested in the word "impossible"—recognizing that its greatest power comes from the inside out. It may appear weak and nimble to the onlooker, but deep beneath the surface it grows, it strengthens, it builds, preparing itself for the unexpected day when it will emerge and rise above all those who bet against it, who questioned its endurance.

February 12th

🍎

Act: Come up with an exciting way to bring awareness to the power of kindness in your school. Make a poster, start a club, or leave random kindness stickers on people's lockers.

Quote: "Getting an idea should be like sitting down on a pin; it should make you jump up and do something." ~**E. L. Simpson**

Reflection: Janice is a student who began her journey into the world of kindness with simple acts of love. What started small grew into a project to spread kindness through the entire school. Janice took to the student's lockers and began to execute her plan; placing ten notes a week in random lockers.

> Hey friend! Always remember that tough times don't last, while tough people do. So don't lose hope when things don't seem good! Keep a little spirit and cheer! Remember that you are not alone; your family and friends are your support systems to fall back on. Keep a smile on your face and stay positive always!
> —Anonymous

It wasn't recognition that drove Janice, but the pure joy of possibly touching someone's heart. Imagine her surprise when a note of gratitude found its way onto the school's confession page on Facebook:

> Dear Anonymous, I received your note in my locker today. I was having a very long and frustrating day that ended very late, and your note cheered me up. Thank you and hope you'll have a great day too!
> —From the locker's owner

February 13th

Act: Spread the love! Start a toy drive with your friends and make a donation to a children's hospital or shelter.

Quote: "Always give without remembering and always receive without forgetting." ~Brian Tracy

Reflection: Every Monday and Friday I would head out with my students on another kindness adventure. It was Chanukah, a time of year in which giving was customary. Our first stop was a local community service organization. We wrapped the gifts and headed out with a list of addresses in our hands and loads of excitement in our hearts. It was a cold December night but the smiles on the faces of the children we visited warmed us to the core.

Abraham and Sara were the last stop on our kindness adventure. Their smiles and the gratitude they expressed were immeasurable, but more than anything it was the appreciation in their mother's eyes as we spent time playing, laughing, and listening to their dreams that gave the experience lasting meaning.

Several years later we made our way back to look for Abraham and Sara, not knowing if they would even remember us. They had moved and we didn't know how we would find them, but we were on a mission and we weren't about to give up. When we finally tracked them down the look on their faces proved the impact we'd had. They had gifted us with a purpose.

February 14th

Act: Going to get your morning coffee? Buy a gift card from the shop and leave it with the barista with an anonymous Valentine's Day note. Ask them to gift it forward to a customer who is particularly friendly that day.

Quote: "Don't judge each day by the harvest you reap but by the seeds that you plant." ~Robert Louis Stevenson

Reflection: One day I stepped into a cafe to charge my cell phone. I saw the barista hand a customer a cup of coffee with a smile and say, "You have a wonderful day now!" I also noticed the silence as the woman took her coffee, walked out, and didn't cast a glance at the barista.

I recognized my opportunity. After all, that is what kindness is: an opportunity. I fumbled within my bag, pulled out a kindness card and handed it to the barista. "This is for you!" She hesitantly took it but as she read the card, her smile returned.

"Tag, you're it! You've been spotted performing an Act of Kindness! Now it's your turn to keep your eyes peeled and pass this along the next time you catch someone in the act!"

With that I handed her a stack of cards. "Pass these along to customers that are particularly kind," I said.

Ignoring kindness can cause one to question whether it matters, and whether they matter. On the other end of the spectrum, it's truly extraordinary how simply acknowledging an act of kindness can and will inspire a person to continue seeking out those opportunities.

February 15th

Act: Buy a dozen sandwiches and pass them out to homeless folks in a busy area. Your act may very well start a domino effect of kindness.

Quote: "If you can't feed a hundred people, then feed just one." ~Mother Teresa

Reflection: For those suffering from homelessness, much of the human interaction they experience is steeped in negativity and they are left feeling forgotten, ignored, and unseen. "Get a job!" "Bum," "Get out of here," and "You're driving down my business," are just some of the common catchphrases thrown their way.

We are all people. Each and every one of us with our own backstory, our own personal struggles, our own hopes and dreams yet to be realized. But each and every one of us also has a choice; a choice that shapes the way we interact with others traveling down their own path.

We can turn our heads and pretend not to see the homeless. Or we can reach out and make a small meaningful connection. It isn't money they are after; it's something far more meaningful and far simpler to dispense—human interaction. A sandwich isn't just a meal to them, it's recognition that they haven't been forgotten, that while many may see them as "bums"—you see them as people.

February 16th

✿

Act: Send a heartfelt, genuine note to your boss or mentor sharing some of the benefits you've gained from the job; not just professionally but personally as well.

Quote: "Remember that you are all people and all people are you." ~Joy Harjo

Reflection: The end of the school year was always tough for me; saying goodbye to yet another extraordinary group of eighth-grade students. I ended each year with lots of hugs, a bunch of happy tears, and a special personalized letter to each student. This year was different than all those before it, though. I wouldn't be returning the following school year. It was time for me to embark on yet another adventure and start my nonprofit Life Vest Inside. As I sat in the library writing away, I thought of one other person who deserved a letter.

The school's principal, Rabbi Schwed, had been part of my life since grade school, when I was his student. Now, as his colleague, I saw beyond his seemingly tough exterior to the depth with which he cared about every student. Being in a position of authority is never easy. With countless complaints and rarely any positive feedback, it can be easy to lose sight of the difference you truly make. I knew one thing for certain, Rabbi Schwed had made a huge difference to me and he deserved to know it. His surprised reaction when I handed him the letter was comical, but there was nothing comical about the words of gratitude he shared with me after reading the note. Rabbi Schwed teared up and said, "We'll miss you. This place most certainly won't be the same without you." His words meant more than he could imagine.

February 17th

✌

Act: Kick-start someone's day. Send them a good-morning text when you wake up.

Quote: "You get the best out of others when you give the best of yourself." ~Harvey S. Firestone

Reflection: We all have those days. From the moment we wake up, the endless list of questions and challenges crosses our worried minds. Am I ready to face another day? How am I going to get it all done? What am I doing with my life? What if I fail? What if?

Hesitantly we grab our cell phones knowing that we need to get up. As we take a deep sigh and open the phone we unexpectedly find an encouraging text message from someone. The length doesn't matter; simply knowing that on that day you were the first person they reached out to leaves you with a warm and fuzzy feeling. Almost instantaneously your energy level shoots to new heights. The questions are silenced as you pop out of bed with a big smile on your face ready and prepared to face the challenges of the day.

February 18th

★

Act: Open your heart and mind to the world. Take a risk and try something new. Scary? Yes. Worth it? Definitely.

Quote: "All our dreams can come true, if we have the courage to pursue them." ~Walt Disney

Reflection: Sometimes it can be scary to try something new, but you'll never know what it's like until you take that leap and give it a chance. This can be trying a new food or getting out of your comfort zone when making friends. Introduce yourself to new people you meet today. Instead of worrying about what they will think of you, smile and take the time to get to know a bit more about them. It's likely that they are just as nervous as you are.

February 19th

Act: Character speaks volumes about a person. Be especially mindful of your ethics, even in what may be constituted as small and insignificant matters.

Quote: "Be more concerned with your character than your reputation, because your character is what you really are, while your reputation is merely what others think you are." ~John Wooden

Reflection: As the years pass, values are lost. Not due to the fact that they no longer apply, but rather the frequent disregard for those precious values has numbed us to praising their great worth. The manner in which we treat others has less to do with what is accepted, praised, or ridiculed, and more to do with what we know to be true in our heart of hearts. Listen to your heart. It will not mislead you. The temporary facade of profit or achievement that may stem from unethical behavior is simply that—a facade. You CAN achieve the most extraordinary feats with nothing more than the arsenal of values and ethics of kindness that we are all inherently given as human beings.

February 20th

Act: Plan a fun outing and spend some quality time with your biological or chosen family. Remember, these are the people who love you unconditionally. That's not what you would call an everyday occurrence.

Quote: "The strength of a family, like the strength of an army, is in its loyalty to each other." ~Mario Puzo

Reflection: For me, family has always been number one. As the years passed our tight-knit cousins crew of six grew into fourteen! Our parents would plan outings from apple picking, to picnics in the park, to a day at the zoo. My brother Joey was twenty years old at the time, the oldest grandson, and tasked with the responsibility of keeping the tradition going regardless of how old we grew and how hectic life became. What started out as a parent-free cousins trip to Great Adventure Amusement park turned into a tradition known as Cousins Day. We promised each other, "No matter how old we get, married with kids and all—we will never forget each other. It's family forever!" I remember having tears in my eyes, hoping that those words would remain true for all time. Over ten years have passed; half the cousins are married with kids, but Cousins Day lives on. It most certainly takes effort but it's worth every bit of it. And remember, it's never too late to start a tradition. It can begin with a simple phone call. Start dialing!

Act: Make a friend their favorite meal or buy a bottle of wine and drink it together. Slowly, with no agenda and no time limit.

Quote: "We're so busy watching out for what's just ahead of us that we don't take time to enjoy where we are." ~Bill Watterson

Reflection: We all fall into the trap. Overscheduling, over-working, overextending ourselves to the point where the simple joys in life need to be penciled into our agendas for worry that they may otherwise be forgotten. But often the most enjoyable moments in our lives aren't the ones we plan. Friendship isn't simply another task on the to-do list. It's made up of the moments of stillness in between the hustle and bustle; moments when the clock stops ticking, the phone stops buzzing, and an alarm doesn't sound warning you it's time to move on to the next task on the endless schedule. Time isn't like wine. It doesn't get better with age. We must live in the moments that make life worth living; moments where we can simply be.

February 22nd

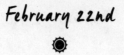

Act: Be honest.

Quote: "If you tell the truth, you don't have to remember anything." ~Mark Twain

Reflection: Remember, constructive criticism and just plain criticism are two diametrically opposing forces. While one encourages growth and strength the other breeds fear, uncertainty, and weakness. Choose your words wisely and help those around you to thrive.

February 23rd

Act: Pay a visit to an animal shelter.

Quote: "The greatness of a nation can be judged by the way its animals are treated." ~Mahatma Gandhi

Reflections: Bring along your children, nieces, nephews, or friends. It's a great way to foster an appreciation for volunteering and animals, and to teach love and compassion. A compassionate person is a kind person. A kind person is a happy person. That is one of the greatest things we can achieve in life.

February 24th

Act: Take the time to visit someone who didn't show up to school today because they were sick. Or make copies of the notes they missed for when they return. No one likes to feel out of the loop.

Quote: "There is no exercise better for the heart than reaching down and lifting people up." ~John Andrew Holmes

Reflection: "Out of sight, out of mind." We may throw this phrase around loosely, but in our heart of hearts we hope that our presence and our absence is felt by those who love us, care for us, and are impacted by us. True kindness stems from seeing beyond yourself and your immediate surroundings. It's reflected in the opportunities to be there for another even in their absence.

February 25th

Act: Drop off dinner or groceries to an elderly friend, neighbor, or relative who can't get out much. You may be the only human contact they have that day.

Quote: "The purpose of life is not to be happy. It is to be useful, to be honorable, to be compassionate, to have it make some difference that you have lived and lived well." ~Ralph Waldo Emerson

Reflection: My former student and I took on an extra food-package delivery one night from our local community food bank. Being a firm believer that everything happens for a reason made it simple to find the beauty in the seemingly disconnected events that transpired that evening. We rang the doorbell several times, but there was no answer. Protocol was to drop it back at the office so that someone would deliver the package the following day. I'm glad that I didn't give up that easily. It was a cold night and there wouldn't have been any reason to feel guilty for not making a second attempt, but instead we tried again. Finally the door opened and there stood Lisa, a middle-aged woman down on her luck. It was clear that Lisa needed more than food. She needed someone to listen.

She told me she was a widow and even though I knew there would be no perfect combination of words I could say to ease the pain of losing her husband, I gave her a platform to openly share her qualms with the way of the world. She wasn't magically healed, but when we walked out of the apartment, she thanked me profusely for reminding her that the world hadn't turned its back on her. There still were those who cared wholeheartedly.

February 26th

Act: See a meter that's about to expire? Surprise the driver and slip in another quarter.

Quote: "Spread love everywhere you go. Let no one ever come to you without leaving happier." ~**Mother Teresa**

Reflection: We all get busy in our hectic everyday lives. Often things can slip our minds. Imagine if we created a culture in which simply being a member of the human race means that someone is looking out for you, that someone has your back even if you may never have met them? If a quarter can create that feeling of possibility in the heart of another, I say sign me up!

February 27th

Act: Adopt a grandfather or grandmother at a local nursing home. Bring a friend and make it part of your routine.

Quote: "It's amazing how much you can learn if your intentions are truly earnest." ~Chuck Berry

Reflection: Every person wants to feel as though their life matters, that their presence matters, and that although they may not live forever, their legacy will continue.

My Saturdays visiting Mr. C. at a local old-age home were the all-time best.

After suffering from a stroke, Mr. C. couldn't speak, but that didn't stop him from opening his doors and his heart to welcome in a group of kids hoping to make his day a bit brighter. Just seeing us interact with one another, catch up on the highlights from the past week, and share stories and anecdotes made him feel at ease. Everyone and anyone was welcomed into Mr. C.'s small apartment. There was a magic to it; no matter how many people stopped by for a visit, there was always room.

Within the four walls of his apartment, lots of friendships were made, some marriages, too, but more than anything was the feeling that we all belonged. That was his legacy.

February 28th

✿

Act: Take the time to get to know something new about a co-worker, or someone you pass by on your way into work. A new friend may be on the horizon.

Quote: "Treat everyone with respect and kindness. Period. No exceptions." ~Kiana Tom

Reflection: As I made my way into the school building for another day of teaching, there he was. Standing six-foot-two with a bright smile on his face and loads of love and hugs to give out to the throngs of students, staff, and administrators he was tasked with protecting. JP isn't just any security guard, he's a friend and a confidant, the person who makes you laugh while you're waiting patiently for your mom to pick you up. We shared stories about his son, stories about my dream of starting Life Vest Inside, stories about inspiring moments, and stories about hardships and failures.

What stood out most about JP was something that not many people had the privilege to see. Next door to the school was a synagogue. Without fail, every morning a car would pull up to the synagogue and JP would rush over, open the door, gently reach his hand out to lift up the elderly man sitting in the front seat, and walk him into the synagogue. I'll never forget the first day I saw this. Turns out the man was paralyzed from the waist down and JP was doing what he knew best—offering a hand and a bit of kindness

Open your eyes and your heart—there's a JP in your midst. Now go ahead and introduce yourself.

March 1st

❧

Act: Laughter is the best mood enhancer. Send a funny picture, video, or article to someone.

Quote: "A little nonsense now and then is cherished by the wisest men." ~Willy Wonka

Reflection: Often it's precisely the moments in which laughter may seem far from appropriate that it's needed most. With its unique ability to momentarily alter a person's mood, laughter lightens the stressful weight we all carry along with us.

You'll find that a shift in a person's mood will not only shift their day, it will positively impact the lives of those they encounter. Like a domino effect, a shift in mood leads to a shift in energy, leads to a shift in possibilities, and leads to a better world.

March 2nd

✦

Act: Take a little extra time to make yourself feel special today. Doll yourself up, make your favorite breakfast, wear your favorite shoes, the list is endless!

Quote: "Love yourself first, and everything else will fall into line." ~Lucille Ball

Reflection: When you feel good on the inside, you radiate a unique aura of positivity that has the power to attract a great deal of endless possibilities into your life. When our world seems chaotic, taking the time to bring order to our appearance does wonders for our inner spirit.

March 3rd

Act: Lend someone money in a dignified manner. We've all been down on our luck. Let's remember, we are here to see each other through.

Quote: "Strive to be the person you needed when you were younger." ~Dr. Laura Miranda

Reflection: Recall the moments when all you were looking for was someone to bet on you, to believe in you, to trust you, and to lend you a hand. When the clouds finally part and the sun begins to shine, it doesn't take much time to lose sight of the moments of desperation that once filled your every day. Don't throw those painful memories out with the trash. You may just find that in time they can be transformed into life teachings, guidance, and strength for someone who is traveling down that same road of misfortune. Overcome the adversity, but don't forget the emotion that accompanied it. The emotion is the secret sauce that allows you to connect, empathize, and empower.

March 4th

🏠

Act: Know of something your child, parent, roommate, spouse, or friend has been wanting for a long time? Leave it wrapped up on their bed for them to find.

Quote: "The best inheritance a parent can give to his children is a few minutes of his time each day." ~O. A. Battista

Reflection: I was sixteen years old when my whole world was turned upside down after a devastating house fire. I would normally find solace in the keys of my piano, but my musical escape went up in the flames. Money was tight, but my dad never made us feel like we were lacking anything. His generosity is unparalleled. With nothing in his pocket he would magically find a way to make you feel like you had the world at your fingertips. There I was, sitting on my bed feeling really low. He knocked on the door, walked in, and without a word carried in a keyboard. Placed it on my bed, smiled, and said, "I know it's not the piano you're used to playing on, but let's see what we can do with it." We sat side by side playing. We didn't say a word but the room was filled to the brim with the sound of true happiness and love.

March 5th

♥

Act: Send an encouraging email to a family member or friend who is embarking on a new endeavor in their lives.

Quote: "I bring you the gift of these four words: I believe in you." ~Blaise Pascal

Reflection: Courage. That's what it takes to pave your own path in spite of the obstacles, challenges, and discouragement thrown your way. I've come to realize that sometimes a person's lack of belief and faith in you or your endeavor is simply a reflection of a lack of belief and faith in themselves.

I've been close to giving up many times in the pursuit of building Life Vest Inside from scratch. But the simple messages of encouragement from people reaching out to share the profound impact the organization has had on their life have empowered me to push forward.

March 6th

Act: Respond to someone when they ask you for a favor.

Quote: "We must all face the choice between what is right and what is easy." ~Albus Dumbledore

Reflection: We're all busy. Between family, work, and other social obligations it's easy to become involved in our own lives, lost within our own little bubbles. Then, out of the blue, when you can't imagine taking on anything additional, comes the request for a favor. It may be a simple request, one that won't take much time, but our minds and bodies are on overload. There are times when we feel as though we're maxed out, that we just can't give anymore. We may put ourselves through a guilt trip; how could we say no, we must seem like such a heartless person. Remember, it's okay to say no, to understand your limits, and know when you need to give a bit to yourself. Giving should never feel like a sacrifice.

A response, even an unfavorable one at that, is better than silence. People are more understanding than we give them credit for.

March 7th

❦

Act: Take extra care to water the plants and flowers in your house.

Quote: "To cultivate a garden is to go hand in hand with Nature in some of her most beautiful processes." ~Christian Nestell Bovee

Reflection: Life is a balancing act. Too much of a good thing can bring unexpected disaster; too little and you fall short of supposed success. Finding the balance is where the challenge exists. Labeling something as good or bad is simply the misconception that things are one way or the other. Our choices and decisions determine the outcome. How will we utilize the gifts we've been given and the challenges we face to produce goodness in all we do, all we see, and in every life we touch?

March 8th

🍎

Act: Is this seat taken? Invite someone who is sitting alone to sit at your lunch table. Don't stick to the status quo.

Quote: "If you go looking for a friend, you're going to find they're very scarce. If you go out to be a friend, you'll find them everywhere." ~Zig Ziglar

Reflection: What better way to get to know someone and break the ice than sharing a meal at the same table?

I remember walking into the lunchroom as a shy, self-conscious, highly awkward loner sophomore. It wasn't easy. We've all been there, regardless of how confident we pretend to be. The walk across the enormous expanse of the high school lunchroom could intimidate anyone, and making the journey alone can be paralyzing. So I ask you, those of you surrounded by the crowd, while you still may not have found your place in the scene, look for "us" in the crowd. The shy, the uncomfortable, the worried, the fearful—but the truly good-hearted. You'll be pleasantly surprised by what you find hiding beneath that seemingly uneasy exterior.

March 9th

Act: Stop by your local community center or nursing home and offer your services.

Quote: "Everybody can be great. Because anybody can serve. You only need a heart full of grace. A soul generated by love." ~Martin Luther King, Jr.

Reflection: Find yourself with a short window in your busy schedule? Don't question if giving of your time in such a small fashion is worthwhile. Act and you'll see that its value is far greater than the yardstick you have been using to measure it.

From volunteering to cook at the soup kitchen, to reading a senior citizen their mail, to engaging in a few moments of conversation, to listening to a story, to simply handing out flyers, there is something for everyone. You have more to offer than you know.

Time is fleeting. But the impact we make within that time is eternal. Instead of seeing time as something that needs to be stored up until the opportune moment to unleash its potential, make the most of those extra minutes. The amount of time we give all at once isn't what determines or measures our impact. Rather, it's the heart, the thought, the love, and the intention we infuse within that short time span. Release yourself from the mindset that giving, or anything for that matter, is an all-or-nothing business. Be realistic with yourself and give what you can. Because the extra minutes you utilize to uplift another adds an exponential value to the time they have left on this earth.

March 10th

Act: Pay the toll for the person behind you (So, wait the extra two minutes and don't use your E-ZPass).

Quote: "It is more rewarding to watch money change the world than watch it accumulate." ~Gloria Steinem

Reflection: Anonymous acts of kindness are often the most rewarding for the giver. It became something of a fun thrill-seeking activity as I crossed the Verrazano Bridge into Staten Island. "This is for the person behind me. And do me a favor—pass this kindness card along to him." The toll collector took the money and Act of Kindness card from my hand, smiled, and nodded his head. I can tell he was super excited to be included in my little experiment of kindness. There's nothing better and more thrilling than seeing the look of shock and wonderment as the next person in the line inches up to the toll booth, only to be told that their toll has been paid. But what excites me more than anything is seeing their first reaction when they grab hold of the card. I drive off hoping that they won't catch me. Just one act of kindness from one member of the human race to another for no reason whatsoever. Simply the satisfaction of making their day brighter and possibly filled with a bit more hope.

It was a week later that I read a small newspaper clipping: A CHAIN OF KINDNESS AT A TOLLBOOTH ON THE HIGHWAY. Apparently the chain continued to be paid forward for over thirty people! Did I start the chain? I'll never know—but then again that's not the point, is it?

Act: Kindly hand your pocket change over to a homeless person. Don't forget to smile and take the extra sixty seconds to introduce yourself and ask them their name. A few short words add an untold value to the change you hand them.

Quote: "If you cannot do great things, do small things in a great way." ~Napoleon Hill

Reflection: Pulling out of a parking spot a while back I spotted a homeless man with a cup in his hands who I would come to know as Bruce. I didn't have any cash on me, only some spare change, but I rolled down the window, called him over and asked how his day had been. "Not so great," he responded, "but doing what I can." I looked him in the eye, smiled, and said, "I don't have much on me but I hope that this can help you out just a bit." As I placed the coins in his paper cup and smiled at him, his eyes opened wide. He pointed his fingers at his eyes and then back at mine. "You can see," he said. It was Bruce that was able to see me. He touched my soul that day.

March 12th

✿

Act: Proclaim today Kindness Day! Plan a kindness activity in your place of work.

Quote: "Happiness is not something that you get in life. Happiness is something you bring to life!" ~Dr. Wayne W. Dyer

Reflection: Working in a facility aimed to help people facing struggles with mental illness is no easy feat, and my friend Jeff understood the importance that positivity played amongst his colleagues. It was easy to get down on yourself when you ran into a roadblock with a patient. Often simply questioning what we can do propels us to find a solution. It may not turn out as planned, but the beauty is in the attempt.

Jeff set to work creating kindness cards: small reminders that kindness is within our reach. You don't need to go looking for it; often it's the things that are right in front of us. Each card with the same message but different meaning for every person whose hands it would pass through.

"You've been tagged by the Random Acts of Kindness Club, making the world better one act of kindness at a time."

Excitedly Jeff brought them to work and began to distribute them. Jeff's effort to bring kindness to his workplace made those who met him, conversed with him, and crossed his path, smile. How can you liven up your workplace?

Act: Gather a group of friends to hand out balloons or flowers to patients in a nearby hospital.

Quote: "Happiness is a perfume you cannot pour on others without getting some on yourself." ~Ralph Waldo Emerson

Reflection: With hearts wide open and gift in hand, I, along with a group of community volunteers, piled out of the bus to the children's ward at the hospital ready and excited to give. As we made our way in, we took a moment to brace ourselves for the flood of emotions we expected to take over our hearts.

My seven-year-old Disney Goofy hat was my all-time favorite costume. It always did the trick and made people smile even in the most dismal situations. Naturally, my Goofy hat made its way to the hospital that very day as I jumped about singing, handing out gifts, and doing all that I could to pass on a bit of cheer. The kids were amazing and the feeling of happiness that accompanied that day was unlike any other. There was one boy in particular I connected with on a different level. His name was Yaakov, and his smile was like a light in the darkness.

As I headed out and said my final goodbyes to Yaakov, I spotted him looking at my Goofy hat and smiling wholeheartedly. Just as we were about to leave, I stopped, ran back, and handed Yaakov the Goofy hat. It served its purpose with me; now it was time to serve another.

March 14th

Act: Be a beacon of positivity. Remember, positive energy doesn't remain stagnant; it has the power to transfer to another and turn their entire day around.

Quote: "Your mind is a powerful thing. When you fill it with positive thoughts your life will start to change." ~Zig Ziglar

Reflection: The energy we put out into the world is very often the same quality of energy reflected back at us. It's no surprise then that when we focus on the negative things, we are met with more hardship and frustration. The most powerful medicine to ease the worries of a stressful day is simply a small shift in perspective. No, it may not be easy amidst the curve balls life throws our way, but it's possible. So, give the world the best you have and the world will find a way to bring the very best back to you.

March 15th

Act: Fight the urge to gossip. Ask yourself, what do you want to be known for?

Quote: "It's better to recall something you wish you'd said than something you wish you hadn't." ~Frank A. Clark

Reflection: Ever wonder why we were gifted two eyes, two ears, two nostrils, but only one mouth? Think of the power of the mouth. Its ability to communicate thoughts, ideas, complex philosophy, and great inspiration. Thoughts are only given power through the great ability of speech, and speech communicates those thoughts in a clear, concise, and well organized manner. We all know the feeling of being tongue-tied. Perhaps we have great thoughts in our head, but if we are unable to communicate them to the world it's hard to see what purpose they serve. The gift of speech is one of man's most powerful tools. Yet that same vessel of power and beauty can, if not used properly, cause a great deal of pain by spreading words of hate, violence, and fear. The more we think about the way we use our voice the more powerful it can truly become. If we taint our mouth with words of falsehood, gossip, and mockery, we taint the same vessel that we hope to call upon to deliver words of meaning, influence, and strength. Perhaps we were gifted with one mouth to remind us that we have but one vessel and we must guard it well.

March 16th

Act: Plan a date with your child or a young person you mentor and spend some alone-time together.

Quote: "While we try to teach our children all about life, our children teach us what life is all about." ~Angela Schwindt

Reflection: On my eleventh birthday, it was pouring rain, dark, and gloomy outside, but my mom and I were still headed to the city for a day out filled with stops at some of my favorite stores, FAO Schwarz being the most exciting of all. I always loved toys—still do! But looking back I realize that it was more exciting to be with one of my favorite people. I remember every detail about that day. It was just Mom and me and I felt like the most important person in her world. To top it all off, she gifted me with what would become my all-time favorite book, *Little Women*. To this very day I still recall the short yet touching inscription she wrote in the front cover of the book: "To my Orly, my 1st daughter, happy 11th birthday! I know you will enjoy this book and I hope it inspires you to continue dreaming."

March 17th

♥

Act: Call or visit a friend or relative who hasn't been feeling well lately. Showing that you care can be very powerful medicine.

Quote: "Too often we underestimate the power of a touch, a smile, a kind word, a listening ear, an honest compliment, or the smallest act of caring, all of which have the potential to turn a life around." ~Leo Buscaglia

Reflection: In giving we are energized, sometimes even more so than the person we are giving to.

When my friend Louis reached out to one of his kindergarten classmates to reminisce about where life's unpaved path had taken them, he was confronted with an opportunity to bring what had started off as a simple act of kindness to the next level. Upon learning that his dear friend's husband had become ill, Louis made his way to the hospital with a birth angel statue. He had never met his classmate's husband before, but a connection was instantly formed. The birth angel symbolized hope, and Louis's gift eventually made it back to the man's house, as did the man, safe and healthy.

March 18th

✺

Act: Compliment someone's smile.

Quote: "A smile is a curve that sets everything straight."
~Phyllis Diller

Reflection: A compliment has the potential to influence a person's mood and shift their day around. Infuse your words with an extra bit of love and watch as it boosts someone's confidence and gives them yet another reason to keep on smiling. Better yet, see the true power of a genuine compliment in a person's eyes. A smile is simply the curvature of the lips, but the heart of a person, their essence, comes through the eyes.

March 19th

Act: Offer to join a neighborhood cleanup effort or, even better, start your very own!

Quote: "Start where you are. Use what you have. Do what you can." ~Arthur Ashe

Reflection: A neighborhood is more than just an area of a city or town, it's the uniqueness and the essence of the neighbors that make it up. It is only once we start seeing beyond our own four walls and recognizing that the stronger the whole, the stronger we will be in turn, that we can transform the word into a living, breathing, and flourishing community. Have an idea that will improve your neighborhood? Start setting it into motion and watch how the support of the community will follow. The first step is the hardest; don't be discouraged if this doesn't run as smoothly as you anticipated. Nothing gets transformed overnight. Your efforts may not be realized today, but they are needed today to leave a lasting impact on tomorrow.

March 20th

🍎

Act: Be brave. Invite someone you don't usually hang out with to make plans over the weekend.

Quote: "Much of the vitality in a friendship lies in the honoring of differences, not simply in the enjoyment of similarities."
~James Fredericks

Reflection: Stepping out of our comfort zone takes courage. Endless "what if"s crowd our minds and fill our subconscious. What if I call and she says no? What if they don't like me? What if I feel stupid?

I invite you to see the other end of the spectrum. What if you make a new best friend? What if you truly connect? What if this friendship leads you to many more? What if you finally feel like you've found someone you can be yourself around?

There's only one way to find out.

Act: Spend some time organizing your closet. Donate clothing, blankets, coats, toys, scarves, and anything in between that you don't use anymore to a local homeless shelter, charity, or religious organization.

Quote: "We think too much and feel too little. More than machinery, we need humanity. More than cleverness, we need kindness and gentleness." ~Charlie Chaplin

Guest Reflection: I had spent weeks gathering donations of food, clothes, blankets, and toiletries to give out to the homeless in the community. When we got there, we began to hand out bottles of water to let people know we were there and what we were doing.

As the donations were being handed out, people began thanking me and telling me their stories. We shared laughs, tears, and hugs. That day I learned the human faces of homelessness. Each person has a story that needs to be told if only we take the time to listen. I wasn't just handing out donations that day, I was handing out dignity and hope. ~Jeff Kuske

March 22nd

Act: Offer someone your seat on the bus or train (try it on a day when you could've used the seat—the experience is quite different).

Quote: "For it is in giving that we receive." ~Saint Francis of Assisi

Reflection: We all have terrible days. Sleeping past the alarm, trouble at the post office, missing the train. There's tension in every inch of your body. And then finally you get a moment of peace as you step onto the train and grab one of the last seats available. You deserve that seat. The train doors fly open and another person walks on, carrying a load on her back, coffee in her hand, and frustration on her face. Then comes the dreaded announcement: "We apologize for the inconvenience as the train will be held at the station until further notice." You look down at the heavy bags in your hand and back at the distraught woman who whispers to herself in anger.

"It looks like you need this seat more than I do." A look of shock flashes on her face as she walks over and takes your seat. A moment later you see it. She takes a deep breath and suddenly you feel the tension in your body subside as you breathe along with her. Perhaps it won't be one of "those days" after all.

March 23rd

Act: Buy a dozen balloons and give them out randomly on the street!

Quote: "A kind heart is a fountain of gladness, making everything in its vicinity freshen into smiles." ~Washington Irving

Reflection: Something about a balloon unquestionably puts a smile on people's faces. Is it a childhood memory? The reminiscence to a time of celebration? Or is it simply what it represents? The more you give of your air supply the stronger it becomes, the higher it rises, lifting the spirits of all those who stare in amazement as it soars higher and higher into the sky.

March 24th

✿

Act: Gather all your coworker's birthdays and create a Birthday Wall.

Quote: "It is lovely, when I forget all birthdays, including my own, to find that somebody remembers me." ~Ellen Glasgow

Reflection: As a teacher working in middle school, birthdays were a big deal! Balloons, birthday cards, cakes, lockers being decorated. But then there would always be a few kids whose birthdays would come and go without a word. It was time to do something about that. Enter the Birthday Wall! An awesome wall my students and I created in the hallway where we would hang a list of all the birthdays for the upcoming month. When it was your birthday, guess whose name would be proudly displayed front and center for all to see? With a birthday card signed by your class and a tasty Dunkin' Donuts muffin, no one would ever feel overlooked again.

March 25th

Act: Leave an inspirational note in your favorite library book before returning it. Your words may be the motivation the next patron was hoping to find.

Quote: "Be an encourager. The world has plenty of critics already." ~Dave Willis

Reflection: Inspiration has a funny way of finding us in the most interesting of times, and sometimes at the most necessary moments. I was once gifted a book in which I found a small note tucked in the pages, a reminder to keep smiling through the unexpected storms life would throw my way. It was only years later in the midst of such a storm that I randomly pulled it from the shelf, immersed myself in its pages, and rediscovered the note. It had always been there, but at that precise moment those words and that note made all the difference.

March 26th

✦

Act: Be honest with yourself and the people around you. It's just as important to be true to yourself as it is to be true to others.

Quote: "You are what you are when nobody is looking." ~Abigail Van Buren

Reflection: Honesty and integrity are the yardsticks by which we measure our intrinsic value. The difficulty lies in our willingness to have the courage to look ourselves in the mirror, remove the endless layers and masks we often clothe ourselves in, and truthfully answer some difficult questions about our true intentions. Only you can know the true intentions of your heart—so listen closely to what it's whispering. Remember, honesty may be the road less traveled, but it is a path worth treading.

March 27th

Act: Leave a collection of positive news clippings in a hospital waiting room.

Quote: "Hope is like a road in the country; there was never a road, but when many people walk on it, the road comes into existence." ~Lin Yutang

Reflection: At first glance it may appear that the hospital hallways and rooms are filled with worry, fear, despair, suffering, anger, and confusion. But with a closer look and attentive ear you'll hear the sounds of love, friendship, and, most important, hope. Hope for a better outcome, hope for a better tomorrow, hope for the simple things. Hope needs its positive reinforcements, its reminders, its signs that even when things seem more dismal than ever—hope surely remains.

March 28th

🏠

Act: Do your parents, grandparents, or elderly friends struggle with technology? Spend some time setting them up and answering any questions they may have about their computers, phones, and social media.

Quote: "We've put more effort into helping folks reach old age than into helping them enjoy it." ~Frank A. Clark

Reflection: The smile on Nana's face and seeing her bop her head to the sounds of her favorite French music was worth every second it took to slowly and clearly go over the steps from turning on her computer to getting online, finding YouTube, and typing in the name of her favorite old-school artist. Nana was ready with pencil and paper in hand, eager to meticulously take notes on every step she would have to take.

In today's fast-paced world of technology, there's always an opportunity to share some newfound knowledge that can make life a bit easier and smoother. But more than the knowledge you provide, people appreciate the time they get to spend with you. One thing is for certain; you'll have some really funny stories to tell the rest of the family after your tech session. That alone is priceless!

Act: At the end of the day, call or text a friend to see how their day went.

Quote: "One of the most beautiful qualities of true friendship is to understand and to be understood." ~Lucius Annaeus Seneca

Reflection: Reaching out stems from the ability we have to reach inward and find the courage to give wholeheartedly. Reaching out without reaching in leaves your gift devoid of its potential strength and capability. Every person wants to be seen and to know that someone is thinking of them. Perhaps wanting to be seen is more a need than a desire. Knowing that you matter to another often lifts us out of those slumps when we question our worth. Remember this: No one, regardless of how confident they appear to be, is exempt from questioning their worth. We all go through it at one point or another. Mere acknowledgment will offer one the strength needed to lift them out of that state of mind.

It's not about the text message, it's about the fact that in the midst of the chaos of your day, you took a moment to think of another in the very same way you hope for someone to think of you. Start seeing your random texts or calls to a friend as little virtual gifts of appreciation and love. You may find that you'll start sending them out more often.

March 30th

Act: Take a few moments to neatly hang up your clothes in a store dressing room.

Quote: "We can do no great things, only small things with great love." ~Mother Teresa

Reflection: My friend was exhausted, drained, and ready to call it a night. Working at a retail store on Black Friday was no ordinary experience and being a newbie made it that much more "extraordinary" to say the least.

When the doors finally closed, he was anxious to get home. Everyone was.

The dreaded announcement came over the intercom, followed by a collective groan, knowing all too well what it meant. "All dressing rooms must be cleaned before any employee can leave."

As he arrived at his assigned dressing room he was shocked and relieved to find an array of pants, shirts, and jackets all neatly hung on hangers and ready to be put back on the racks. What would have easily taken several hours took only moments. He would never know who was responsible, but he'll always remember the impact it made.

March 31st

❧

Act: Clean up the graffiti in your neighborhood or another nearby location.

Quote: "Creativity is allowing yourself to make mistakes. Art is knowing which ones to keep." ~Scott Adams

Reflection: See the goodness in the world, the beauty, the artistry, and the magic within the signs you pass by on your morning stroll, your walk to the bus, your drive home from work, and your casual jog to the beach.

Connect with a few local artists and perhaps find a way to turn ordinary graffiti into a beautiful, masterful work of art and inspiration.

Whenever I find myself questioning the way of the world, pondering my place within it all, and contemplating the next choice to make, I cast my eyes to the seemingly ordinary around me; the signs within the everyday experiences. Often the harder we look for the solution, the more it escapes us. Answers can be found in the most unlikely of places, and there's nothing more unlikely than right before your very eyes.

April 1st

Act: Clean the inside of your desk before you leave class. You might just start a trend.

Quote: "We are what we repeatedly do. Excellence, then, is not an act, but a habit." ~Aristotle

Reflection: We're all familiar with the phrase "Cleanliness is next to godliness." The question is, why? The simple exertion of time and care on our part to keep a space we're gifted to occupy speaks volumes about our character.

April 2nd

Act: Start a collection for your local food bank at your office or a community store. For many, the need for food is year round, not just during the holidays.

Quote: "While earning your daily bread, be sure you share a slice with those less fortunate." ~H. Jackson Brown, Jr.

Reflection: A community is only as amazing as the people who form it. Recognizing the unseen hardships that people face struggling to afford the essential groceries and put a meal on the table is key to the overall health of any community. It means everything when members of a community rise up to fill the need, to ensure that no person feels abandoned. In my community hundreds of women, with no reason aside from the desire to give, dedicate hours of their week preparing delicious food for those less fortunate. Whether you cooked, baked, or simply delivered a meal and engaged in a few words of meaningful conversation, every job was important, every person important, every interaction important.

My sister did this every week. She didn't know it, but I was proud of her. Meticulous with every cookie she baked, every package she wrapped. It wasn't simply about the meal, but the way it was presented, the dignity in which it was given, the heart she infused into every ingredient she added. But more than anything it was the lives of the people she touched with every visit.

April 3rd

Act: Hold the train door open for someone rushing to get in (be careful, kindness doesn't mean risking your life). We all know the terrible feeling of running to the train only to have the doors slam shut right before we enter.

Quote: "We can't help everyone, but everyone can help someone." ~Ronald Reagan

Reflection: It's true what they say: When one door closes another door opens. But when you find yourself in a rush, something as simple as a door staying open for a split second can be the difference between a sigh of grief and a sigh of relief.

April 4th

Act: Next time you're at the grocery store and someone is short on change, offer to give them what little you can. It happens to the best of us.

Quote: "A man is great by deeds, not by birth." ~Chanakya

Guest Reflection: I noticed her almost immediately. Standing at the front of the checkout line buying diapers and baby formula among other things. She swiped her debit card. The look of despair when the word "declined" popped up on the screen was heartbreaking. She swiped it again and again; no change. I heard grumbling behind me as tears began to well in her eyes.

The entire line fell silent as an elderly woman stepped up behind her and whispered, "Don't worry, dear, your baby will get what she needs." She handed a card to the cashier and paid the entire bill. I don't think there was a dry eye in the line. We all left the supermarket that day with more than just groceries, but a lesson that would stay with us; it stayed with me. We may not know each other's names or stories, but we're here to see each other through; to instill hope when it seems as though hope is lost. ~Jeff Kuske

April 5th

✿

Act: We all make mistakes. Today, practice a bit more patience with your coworkers, recognizing that we're all human.

Quote: "To err on the side of kindness is seldom an error." ~Liz Armbruster

Make-a-Choice Reflection

You have an important meeting at the end of the day and you assign one simple task to a coworker. "Please print the packet for today's meeting and get it to me by 4:00 pm!" At 3:55 pm, she runs into the office to hand you the packet, but she printed the old version.

Scenario #1:

"I asked you for one thing! I have had it with your constant mistakes." She feels terrible and will likely doubt every decision she makes moving forward. You're left with a fleeting sense of relief for releasing the tension of a stressful day, but are still not equipped with your packet and head to the meeting frustrated and defeated.

Scenario #2:

You realize that she knows how important this was and how stressed you've been. Her goal was to bring the stress level down, not increase it. "I know you didn't intentionally misprint the packet. I also know that you'll be more mindful in the future."

A mere packet won't destroy you but giving into anger can do just that. Every day we are faced with choices. We cannot change what has already happened, but we have the power to determine our next move.

April 6th

❧

Act: The next time someone asks you for a favor, say yes without hesitation.

Quote: "Be kind whenever possible. It is always possible." ~The Dalai Lama

Reflection: We won't always see or know the impression our actions have made on the life of another—the fleeting inspiration that caused them to be a bit kinder, to be a bit more thoughtful, to put a bit more of themselves out into the world. The story, the incident, the random moment when it all changed for them; when the darkness was suddenly lifted and they could finally see the light; when something ordinary and often overlooked took on a greater meaning for them and suddenly their life was never the same again.

We won't always see or know the impression our actions have made on the life of another, but we do know the impression someone's actions have left on us. Become the hidden catalyst of inspiration.

April 7th

⭐

Act: You are your biggest critic. Quiet the negative, discouraging voices in your head telling you "you can't." You most certainly can because you are amazing just the way you are.

Quote: "Whether you think you can, or you think you can't—you're right." ~Henry Ford

Reflection: The truth is what you proclaim. Your negative thoughts can have a way of destroying you. Don't allow them to occupy your mind, to occupy your heart or to occupy your soul. Bet on yourself a bit more for everyone's sake. Your successes are everyone's success—we are all connected.

April 8th

Act: Make an effort to be genuinely happy for the success and accomplishments of others. We all have our strengths and our weaknesses, but we must always remember to compare ourselves to none other than the person staring at us in the mirror.

Quote: "Success is attaining your dream while helping others to benefit from that dream materializing." ~Sugar Ray Leonard

Reflection: The world is filled with abundance and plenitude. It is a misconception that when one person succeeds, another must fail. By practicing happiness—true happiness—the universe will have no choice but to provide you with more reasons to be happy. Warning: Hardships will come your way as they do for everyone. It is our reaction and ability to see the hidden gemstones of goodness amongst the pain that truly defines us and determines our genuine level of happiness and contentment with the lot we've been given.

April 9th

🏠

Act: Take the initiative and fix something in your home that has been broken for a while. Perhaps set up a time to work on it as a group.

Quote: "Initiative is doing the right thing without being told."
~Victor Hugo

Reflection: I'll never forget how terrified my mom would be walking downstairs to see the basement in a few inches of water and beginning the long, exhausting, and tedious process of draining the water and cleaning the floor. No matter how many times it happened, my mom always took the initiative, but you could tell it drained her.

One rainy summer night, I had just gotten home from a two-hour drive. It was midnight and I was exhausted. My family was away and getting back the very next morning. As I walked into the house, I heard the dreaded noise—dripping! The basement was under two inches of water. I had a choice. Spend an hour cleaning it up or head to bed knowing full well that my mom would deal with it in the morning. I could say I didn't see it; after all it was in the basement. I took an extra moment and pictured my mom's frustration walking into a flooded basement. Suddenly, there was no choice to be made. I never did tell my mom about the flood that evening.

April 10th

♥

Act: Show a bit of extra affection to a loved one.

Quote: "Love is not to be purchased, and affection has no price." ~St. Jerome

Reflection: Sometimes all it takes is a hug, a touch on the arm, a kiss on the cheek, or a squeeze of the shoulders to make someone feel supported and comforted. You'll find that the givers of affection get as much satisfaction as those who receive it. Go ahead; make someone feel great.

April 11th

◉

Act: Help out in the kitchen after dinner tonight. Offer to do the dishes, condense the leftovers, or take out the trash.

Quote: "There are no traffic jams when you go the extra mile." ~Roger Staubach

Reflection: Often the simplest forms of kindness fly under the radar, never categorized as kindness at all. But being kind doesn't mean you need to go looking for opportunities to engage in positive activities; it simply means seeing the everyday opportunities that have always been there passing you by unnoticed. You may not be applauded for days on end or receive acknowledgment all together, but kindness in its purest form enjoys the anonymity and the hidden pleasure of knowing it made someone's day a little bit brighter.

April 12th

Act: Start educating yourself about Earth Day and make a commitment to celebrate this year in your very own special way.

Quote: "The environment is where we all meet; where all have a mutual interest; it is the one thing that we all share." ~Lady Bird Johnson

Reflection: One hundred ninety-six countries, over seven billion people; a world filled with differences—differences in culture, ethnicity, religion, skin color, gender, beliefs, sexuality, hopes, dreams—but amidst the multitude of differences, one world, one earth, one planet houses us all. Setting aside the differences that divide, let's utilize the differences that unite: differences in talents, skills, capabilities, and creativity. The time has come to save "our" earth, remembering that the well-being of the world doesn't cast bias, it sees us for the one body we truly are. Separately, we may succeed, but together we are in for a surefire victory, a triumph like no other. We only have one earth—let's celebrate it.

April 13th

🍎

Act: Start a birthday calendar for the staff at your school.

Quote: "As a rule I always look for what others ignore." ~Marshall McLuhan

Reflection: From students, to staff, to one of my all-time favorite janitors—the Birthday Wall we had at the Yeshivah of Flatbush proved to be a huge success! One day one of the school principals said jokingly, "Orly, you know, I feel a bit left out. My birthday is August 25th and there's no school in the summertime!" It wasn't a joke to me. "You can expect a phone call from me on August 25th," I said with a big smile. From the look on his face I knew that he thought I would forget.

He answered his phone on the morning of August 25th to a terrible rendition of "Happy Birthday" sung by yours truly. I felt his smile through the phone. Mission accomplished.

April 14th

Act: Offer to run an errand for someone in your life who's strapped for time.

Quote: "Seek to do good, and you will find that happiness will run after you." ~James Freeman Clarke

Reflection: Parenthood is no simple task. Time is no longer your own; it's in the hands of someone you care for more deeply than you will ever care for yourself. It may not be easy, but it afforded my cousin Ronette the opportunity to tap into skills and talents she never knew she had. Making a transition from a life in which time can be spent how you choose to a life in which your time is no longer yours is no easy feat. One can easily lose themselves and their identity by forgetting the importance of balance and the need to give to themselves.

It was Ronette's husband Joey's day off. When Joey offered to spend the day with baby Ralph, Ronette immediately saw the free time as an opportunity to take care of odds and ends in the house she couldn't tend to with Ralph in one arm. It came as quite a shock when Joey stopped her, and said, "This is a day for you. Whether you want to go for lunch, get a manicure, or get some much needed sleep. Today is about giving to yourself." What a foreign concept, but it was only once she paused and took him up on his offer that she realized just how important it was and just how grateful she was for a husband who gifted her with something super valuable—time.

April 15th

Act: Bring along an extra apple or banana as you head out today. An opportunity will undoubtedly present itself to share your healthy treat with another!

Quote: "If the world seems cold to you, kindle fires to warm it." ~Lucy Larcom

Reflection: My friend Jeff didn't see himself as a hero, but then again he didn't see himself through the eyes of those whose lives he touched simply by being himself. To Jeff, stashing a bag filled with extra treats in his bottom right drawer at work on the off chance that someone may have forgotten their lunch or needed an extra boost of energy during a long, draining workday was something that was simply part of his DNA.

Go the extra mile. Expect the unexpected. Be mindful of the needs of others as much as you're mindful of your own. The bag of goodies may have gone back and forth with him to work one hundred times or more as it patiently awaited the moment when it could be put to good use. For Jeff, one time out of a hundred was all he needed.

April 16th

Act: Give a genuine compliment to those you hardly know but often pass.

Quote: "Compliments cost nothing, yet many pay dear for them." ~Thomas Fuller

Reflection: Criticism and praise may seem like opposite ends of the spectrum, but commonality exists within the impact they make on another's life. Sometimes, regardless of our best efforts, others will find fault in our actions. While a great achievement can be deflated by a few disparaging words, several words of appreciation and gratitude can instantaneously lift someone out of a frustrating situation and give them the motivation to keep pushing forward. We all have the ability to be a catalyst for positive inspiration. You'll find that when lifting up another you will inadvertently lift yourself.

Let's train our eyes to see the goodness within everyone and everything. Before we know it, goodness will become more readily seen.

April 17th

✿

Act: Next time you go to a coffee shop, grab an extra cup for a coworker. A hot cup of coffee can be all that's needed to melt a cold, tough exterior.

Quote: "Constant kindness can accomplish much. As the sun makes ice melt, kindness causes misunderstanding, mistrust, and hostility to evaporate." ~Albert Schweitzer

Reflection: Being thoughtful isn't a requirement, but it's precisely the act of thoughtfulness that sets you apart from the rest. It's seeing beyond what a person shows you to what a person hopes you'll see all on your own. It's the small gestures that take you by surprise, make you smile, touch your heart, and magically inspire you to seek out ways to make someone feel just as great. Sometimes a dose of thoughtfulness extended to someone who may be far from thoughtful can give a positive spin to the uneasy relationship dynamic that has been present for longer than you care to imagine.

Be different. Be bold. Be brave. Be thoughtful.

April 18th

❦

Act: Drop off a wholesome dinner to an exhausted, over-whelmed parent. Include a note letting him or her know that they are doing a fantastic job!

Quote: "We make a living by what we get, but we make a life by what we give." ~Winston Churchill

Reflection: Parenthood is the purest form of love and kindness. In an instant your life is no longer your own. Suddenly the wants and needs of another become your greatest concern and worry. For those who have not yet traveled down that path it may seem as though it's the greatest sacrifice one can make. In fact, it's far from it. Not an obligation, not a sacrifice; a privilege, a lifelong gift, a unique opportunity to leave a lasting impression on the world. It doesn't require a degree, a finite list of skill sets or talents, and is indifferent to one's level of fame or fortune.

It simply requires love.

Be the fuel propelling a parent forward and you, too, will have a hand in the lifelong impact they will make on the lives of their children.

April 19th

✦

Act: Ask for help. Don't be afraid! Sometimes the mere act of seeking advice and guidance has the power to solve our problems. Remember, you were never meant to do everything alone.

Quote: "It is true that no one can harm the person who wears armor. But no one can help him either." ~Kristin Hunter

Reflection: The fear of rejection has the ability to prevent us from taking the necessary steps and leaps to be able to achieve the greatness we were meant to achieve in our lives. By asking for help you're not admitting defeat, you're acknowledging that only through the combined efforts of people seeking an ultimate purpose can something truly great be accomplished. Asking isn't an indication of weakness, vulnerability isn't an indication of weakness. It's the sign of true strength.

Act: Decide to act honestly in any and all business dealings. Your integrity is more important than any personal gain.

Quote: "Don't compromise yourself. You are all you've got."
~Janis Joplin

Reflection: It's your trademark. Your greatest and most valuable possession. It takes years to build, but only moments to destroy. It's not your fortune or fame. It's not measured in dollar signs or your social media following. It's your name and integrity.

Honesty isn't a switch accompanied with the freedom to turn it on and off as we please. Applicable in the moments we need it and dismissible in the moments when we think it doesn't serve our best interest. Honesty is something to live by, to set your life to; your north star amidst the chaos and deception that can often penetrate our world.

Cast off the false belief that one must cheat in order to climb the ladder of success. Choosing to be honest is success in and of itself.

🏠

Act: Slip a gratitude note under your parent's, sibling's, or roommate's door. Who said that gratitude is only reserved for birthdays or special occasions? You may end up finding that the coolest pen pal has been living under the same roof all along.

Quote: "Families are the compass that guides us. They are the inspiration to reach great heights, and our comfort when we occasionally falter." ~Brad Henry

Reflection: As I rummaged through some of my memory boxes, I found a pile of notes from my baby sister. It was our secret way of communicating and wow, how great it made me feel knowing that my sis was looking up to me.

With her chubby little fingers and colorful pen she scribbled her most urgent message on one, two, or even three Post-It notes, crept up to my door, slid them under, and ran back to her room excited to get a response from her big sister.

"Orly, I just wanted to say hi! I miss you and you're out until late almost every night. I needed your advice about a boy in my grade that I really like. Write back to me, sis. Thanks, you're the best!" ~Danielle, your sister.

I often wonder if she ever knew how much I looked forward to those spontaneous colorful notes.

April 22nd

♥

Act: Spend some quality time with friends.

Quote: "The time you enjoy wasting is not wasted time." ~Bertrand Russell

Reflection: There will always be an endless list of tasks on our to-do list. Friends should never be added to a list. It's precisely when we become accustomed to doing so that they fall to the very bottom. You'll find that a bit of rest and relaxation with friends infuses you with the enthusiasm, clear mind, and motivation to power through the "endless list" once you step back into work mode. Friendship isn't a sacrifice; it's a privilege.

April 23rd

Act: See someone having a rainy day? Be their umbrella. Sometimes a person just needs a shoulder to cry on. They may not open up at first, but don't be put off—simply try again.

Quote: "Sometimes someone says something really small, and it just fits right into this empty place in your heart." ~*My So-Called Life*

Guest Reflection: I was just settling down to a plate of spaghetti and a new movie when I saw the caller ID.

Orly was always very cheery, the most optimistic person I knew. So when I heard uncontrollable sobbing on the other end of the phone the alarms went off. After several minutes, she calmed down as I coached her to take deep breaths along with me. I was generally the one pouring my heart out, but I had the unexpected opportunity to be on the receiving end. She didn't expect me to magically fix anything, she just needed to unload and it made me feel so grateful knowing that she had chosen me to be her listening ear. After an almost two-hour call she felt a greater sense of calm and began to laugh again. It wasn't simply a resolution of the evening's troubles, but the understanding that I would be there for her, good times or bad. The optimistic person I knew was finally back. ~Jeff Kuske

April 24th

Act: Adopt a pet from an animal shelter. There are so many pets that would love a place to call home.

Quote: "It's not the size of the dog in the fight, it's the size of the fight in the dog." ~Mark Twain

Reflection: Even animals sometimes feel scared and alone and suffer from abandonment. The next time you are looking to get a pet from a breeder, think twice and visit your local animal shelter first. You may just find the perfect friend.

April 25th

Act: Have a little patience. It goes a long way. And remember, practice makes perfect.

Quote: "Patience and perseverance have a magical effect before which difficulties disappear and obstacles vanish." ~John Quincy Adams

Reflection: "Everything happens in its time" may be a great maxim to live by, but while entrenched in the midst of the frenzy of life it can be challenging and daunting to recall such a prized motto with ease. Disappointment and absence of patience often stem from our lack of understanding that the journey, the process, and the seemingly tough times are indications of failure. While one may master the ability to extend patience to the outside world, it's our ability to grant such a coveted prize to oneself that indicates the ultimate understanding of the importance of patience. You will achieve your greatest dreams with just a bit more faith and patience with yourself. If you try, you'll never fail. The simple ability to try is in itself a huge success.

April 26th

🌍

Act: Praise a local business or restaurant for services well received today. Visit a company's website or write a comment on Yelp. Positive reinforcement should be shared.

Quote: "The real voyage of discovery consists not in seeking new landscapes, but in having new eyes." ~Marcel Proust

Reflection: At a friend's office, the Wall of Shame was a compilation of negative reviews, negative feedback, negative emails posted for all the coworkers to see. Every day it stared them in the eye bringing them down, antagonizing them, picking at their flaws and failures. Perhaps management thought it would inspire them to reach for more, but negativity rarely does the trick and Ann, one of the employees, knew that all too well. She was a great worker, the best. But her capabilities to get the job done weren't what set her apart; it was the constant smile on her face, the warmth emanating from her heart, and her ability to see people the way she knew they deserved to be seen. Some people make the best of a bad situation, and then there are those special individuals who strive to make it better. And Ann was definitely special.

With every positive review posted on Yelp, every praiseworthy note a customer left, Ann smiled as she pinned it on her very own special wall: the Wall of Praise. With every post, morale was lifted, and throughout the store Ann could hear coworkers praising one another for a job well done. It wasn't long before the Wall of Shame forfeited its place in the store and its place in the employees' hearts.

April 27th

Act: Heading out for a drive? On your way to town? Offer to give a friend a lift.

Quote: "Because that's what kindness is. It's not doing something for someone else because they can't, but because you can." ~Andrew Iskander

Reflection: There will never be an end to our to-do lists. The more we cross things off, the faster additional tasks seem to pop up. If we continuously wait for the opportune moment to slow down, stop, and reconnect with those in our lives who may have slipped through the cracks during our pursuit of happiness, the time will continue to escape us. I've found that some of the most meaningful time I've spent with people isn't the hour-long sessions that we needed to schedule way in advance, consulting with calendars and secretaries, but rather the spontaneous moments. The unplanned trip to the supermarket, the impromptu run to the mall, the random drive to grab a bagel. The moments we spend journeying to the next stop may serve as more valuable time than we initially anticipated. So, the next time you head into your car . . . make it count!

April 28th

Act: Buy a lottery ticket and randomly gift it to someone on the street. Hey, you never know!

Quote: "We cannot possibly let ourselves get frozen into regarding everyone we do not know as an absolute stranger." ~Albert Schweitzer

Reflection: I was having a tough time, feeling pressure from my family and my surroundings to be what they defined as "successful." But success isn't simply measured by how much money we acquire, but by the lives we touch. With only a few hundred dollars left in the bank and what felt like the weight of the world on my shoulders, I thought I was alone, I thought no one saw me. I took a deep breath, picked myself back up as I always did, and headed out to face the rest of my day.

In the midst of doing an errand my friend Mordechai ran in, handed me a paper bag, gave me a hug, and ran right out without a word. Written on the outside of the bag was a note: "Orly, just know that you have a whole lotta awesome, kind, amazing qualities and life accomplishments no matter who notices them!" As I read the words on the paper bag, I smiled, and knew that it would all be okay. I opened the bag to find a lottery ticket. It wasn't a winner, but I sure felt like one. The ticket is long gone, but that paper bag is taped to my wall; a reminder that on that day I did in fact win the lottery. Turns out that the real winning ticket in life isn't one that you can exchange for cash or credit. It's knowing that someone sees you at times when you feel invisible.

April 29th

✿✿

Act: The most beautiful forms of kindness happen in the midst of the everyday rush! Don't be so quick to hit the close-door button on the elevator. Keep your eyes peeled for someone rushing to make it—one day that could be you!

Quote: "If you think about what you ought to do for other people, your character will take care of itself." ~Woodrow Wilson

Reflection: Holding the elevator open when you're not in a rush is great; holding it open when you're running late to a big meeting, a concert, to catch a train—now that's kindness.

You won't remember how those extra thirty seconds of time you lost from holding the elevator doors open as someone hopefully dashed to make it would have benefited you, but you can bet that they will retell their kindness story with such excitement. Your story will live on in their heart and amazingly enough in the hearts of those who hear it.

April 30th

🦋

Act: Check in on a friend who has recently lost a loved one. It's not about what you say, it's simply about being there.

Quote: "Walking with a friend in the dark is better than walking alone in the light." ~Helen Keller

Reflection: It may very well be the most difficult challenge we face in our lives: the loss of a loved one. How will we go on without them? Who will be there for us in their place? There are no perfect words to heal the pain, but sometimes words aren't required at all. Your very presence can be all the comfort that is needed.

With the passing of her brother, Rosie's world came crashing down. Joe was her everything and now he was gone and she felt a piece of herself die with him. He was the one she would call in the midst of the everyday chaos. Who would she call without him?

When Rosie's friend Jeff heard the despair on the other end of the line, he knew what she needed: a listening ear. And so he listened. Jeff knew what it was like to feel alone and he vowed to never allow someone to feel that same pain. No one could replace Joe, but Rosie was no longer alone. What began as one person reaching out to another flourished into a friendship that grows with each passing day.

It may very well be the most difficult challenge we face in our lives. Be the reason someone doesn't have to face it alone.

May 1st

✦

Act: Take a few minutes each day to thank God for all the amazing things He bestows on you. If you aren't religious, thanking those around you or sending up an anonymous thank-you can be just as powerful.

Quote: "Only God can turn a mess into a message, a test into a testimony, a trial into a triumph, and a victim into a victory." ~Nishan Panwar

Reflection: Every day, without fail, He bets on you. Rooting for you, believing in you, cheering you on against all odds. You may have failed thousands of times before. Let yourself down, let others down. But, you'll never let Him down. He won't have it. He won't believe it. He won't accept it. You may not see it just yet, but you are here for a reason, for a purpose, to fill a need in this world that only you can fill. You may have decided to give up on yourself, call it quits, throw in the towel, but with every breath you take—let that be a testament that the work is not done, that you have feats yet to be accomplished, goals yet to be realized, dreams yet to be pursued. The world may be betting against you, but remember: He is standing right by your side, seeing you for who you can be as opposed to what you feel like. So when you're afraid and feel as though you can no longer go on, cast your hand out and grab hold; He'll guide you the rest of the way.

Often the hardships in life help us discover and unleash an inner strength that we would never have otherwise stumbled upon. Trust the process; there is order in the chaos. Just believe.

May 2nd

Act: Encourage someone to pursue their lifelong dream or accomplish a goal they set for themselves. First step: Believe they can.

Quote: "There are two kinds of people in the world: those who come into a room and say, 'Here I am!' and those who come in and say, 'Ah, there you are!'" ~Frederick L. Collins

Reflection: Being a motivating force once someone has overcome the initial hurdles of achieving their goal is one thing; empowering them when their future is still unclear, uncertain, and seemingly unrealistic is another. Often those closest to us have a hard time getting behind our dream at the ground level; when we need it most, when it counts most, and when one failed attempt after the other has forced us to question our capability to make it a reality, question whether we were really meant for greatness. But it's precisely those moments and those people that stick around, refusing to allow you to throw away your dream, that ensure you will go the distance. It's not during the thunderous applause, but the awkward and uncomfortable silence when support is needed at its utmost.

May 3rd

🏠

Act: Spend some extra time cleaning up around the house. A clean and fresh space leads to a clean and fresh start in other aspects of your life.

Quote: "As you grow older, you will discover that you have two hands, one for helping yourself, the other for helping others."
~Audrey Hepburn

Reflections: We all have that one thing we've been meaning to clean, organize, or straighten up in our house. In my childhood home it was the office. Well, I'm not quite sure you would call it that. It was more like the room you stored everything in you didn't want to deal with. I couldn't begin to understand how my dad managed to work in such a messy and unorganized space. Being that I was an obsessively organized person, my dad asked me in the past to help him tidy things up, but it seemed like such a daunting task that I was never fully prepared to begin and set aside the amount of time it needed. Finally I decided that one hour is better than nothing, so I went off to the office to begin sorting through the mountains of papers and garbage that accumulated over the course of the years. Little by little the mountains of papers disappeared and what was left was an actual office! I'll never forget my dad's face when he first walked in—it was a complete transformation. Lucky for me, several months later I left my job to start Life Vest Inside. I knew I would need to find a place in the house to get work done and so I went to the newly cleaned office. Those hours cleaning paid off in more ways than one.

May 4th

♥

Act: Call someone you haven't spoken to in a while and let them know that you miss them.

Quote: "Twenty years from now you will be more disappointed by the things you didn't do than by the ones you did do." ~Mark Twain

Reflection: True friendship has a way of bridging the gap between the countless days gone by. It magically turns the long silence into nothing more than a momentary pause, and fills it with laughter and shared memories. Don't allow the fear of being forgotten prevent you from picking up the phone and making an attempt to reconnect. Friendship is never about waiting for someone to make the first move; it's about taking your guard down to allow moments of deep connection to arise. Why hold onto precedence when an amazing friendship hangs in the balance?

May 5th

Act: Be strong, be brave, and forgive. We all make mistakes. Recognizing our own flaws allows us to let go of anger and resentment.

Quote: "When you forgive, you in no way change the past—but you sure do change the future." ~Bernard Meltzer

Reflection: It's one thing to advise another not to harp on their mistakes and let go of the belief that they define who they are and what they will become. It's an entirely different exercise to heed those words of wisdom ourselves.

Cast off the harsh criticism you so readily place on yourself and see the steps you've taken, the ways in which you've grown, the obstacles you've overcome, and the accomplishments you've achieved. Our decisions and choices do bring with them certain repercussions and consequences, but allowing those decisions to dictate the rest of our life story is most dangerous. You are given a pen and pad each day; how you choose to write your story is entirely up to you. You can see it as a continuous novel where your character is given a definite role that can't be altered or see each day as its own separate chapter, building toward a triumphant finish.

May 6th

❧

Act: Feed the birds.

Quote: "Think of the beauty still left around you and be happy." ~Anne Frank

Reflection: Opportunities exist around every corner; the question is whether we take the time to notice.

Who would have thought that a run to the pet shop would bring with it an unexpected ritual that would follow my friend Joshyn throughout his life? As he made his way home with a nice selection of cans of food for his lovely Burmese kittens; some peanuts for Boo, the lively squirrel that made a daily visit to his door; and a small bag of fresh seeds for his two parakeets, Buddy and Woot, something caught his attention.

Having a keen awareness of nature's beauty and presence all around us, his eyes spotted a wandering flock of pigeons. As it normally did, kindness made its way into his mind and into his heart unannounced, all at once, and determined to leave its mark.

The bag of seeds in the backseat of his car was impossible to ignore. With an empty cup in his hand he began scattering cups full of seeds on the ground to share with the pigeons.

It's the immense feeling of happiness that accompanies any act of giving that inspires Joshyn to continue sharing bits of kindness here and there as he goes about his daily routine.

May 7th

🍎

Act: Listen in class. You just may learn something new. And remember, your teachers love you more than you know.

Quote: "Wisdom is the reward you get for a lifetime of listening when you'd have preferred to talk." ~Doug Larson

Reflection: What is the difference between listening and hearing? Hearing is simply the act of perceiving sound through the ear. If you don't have a hearing impairment, hearing naturally just happens. However, listening is something entirely different, requiring concentration to allow the brain to process meaning from the words and sentences being spoken. One must consciously choose to listen. It's through the power of truly listening that one is lead to profound knowledge and understanding.

A hearing impairment is a tragedy; a listening impairment is a shame. So, keep your ears tuned in and begin to hear the countless words of wisdom worth listening to.

Act: Stop by your local bagel store at the end of their workday and ask them to donate leftover bagels. Drop them off at a homeless shelter or soup kitchen.

Quote: "Kindness to me is not a duty or responsibility; it's a unique feeling which makes you happier as you share it." ~Aashish Jagini

Reflection: Aashish wasn't one to give up when a challenge presented itself. This was a lesson he learned all too well during his time working at his family's restaurant in India.

Aashish saw the amount of leftover food that was being discarded at the restaurant while others lay awake at night suffering from hunger pangs. Aashish took it upon himself to find an orphanage in close proximity to the restaurant, but without the means to transport the food and the containers to store it. It looked as though Aashish's hope to make use of the food would simply go down as a lesson in good intentions. But he continued to push forward and arrange for outside transportation and containers.

When Aashish picked up the phone the very next day the voice on the other end filled him with the ultimate satisfaction. "It was the best food they've had in a really long time."

May 9th

Act: Offer to help a tourist find their way.

Quote: "He who gives when he is asked has waited too long."
~Lucius Annaeus Seneca

Reflection: New cities and towns can be confusing. We've all been lost before—physically, emotionally, spiritually. What's more, we all know the great feeling of relief when someone else takes the time to help us find our way or simply points us in the right direction. You just may set a kindness precedent.

Act: Leave an inspirational book on a bus or train with a small inscription letting the finder know that it was in fact waiting for them. You'll never know just how far the book will travel and how many hearts it will touch.

Quote: "There is more treasure in books than in all the pirate's loot on Treasure Island." ~Walt Disney

Reflection: We're all in search of a sign, a reminder, a symbolic clue pointing us in the "right" direction, giving us clarity and reassuring us that there is good news to come in the days ahead.

A chance encounter with an unexpected message, an unexpected book, or an unexpected sign is often the very same words we know in our hearts to be true. We have difficulty in trusting their validity but oddly enough those same words uttered by another, seen on a bumper sticker of a car, spray-painted on a building, or etched into a book we find can be the validity we were seeking to follow our heart.

May 11th

✿✿

Act: Allow a coworker's child to shadow you for a day and learn about your job. They might actually want to follow in your footsteps.

Quote: "When you give someone your time you are giving them a portion of your life that you'll never get back. That is why the greatest gift you can give someone is your time." ~Rick Warren

Reflection: Who we are says way more about us than what we do. Integrate kindness, compassion, and love into your work and you have the ability to inspire anyone to follow in your career path. Seize the opportunity to serve as a mentor and role model to a child just setting off on the path of pursuing their dream. Yes, they will learn a great deal from you, but I can guarantee that you will learn just as much from them. We all need a reminder of why our jobs and the work we do matters. All it takes is a glimpse from the eyes of a child.

May 12th

Act: Take a few minutes to write a handwritten letter to someone who has made a difference in your life.

Quote: "Those who bring sunshine to the lives of others cannot keep it from themselves." ~James Matthew Barrie

Reflection: Spoken words deliver an immediate and powerful impact, but the written word can be called upon again and again at times when words of encouragement and love are needed most. A physical testament reminding us that we did in fact make a difference in spite of the excessive criticism we feed ourselves. A former student of mine once returned a note I'd given her upon her eighth-grade graduation years before. She placed it in my hands and said, "You have made a difference, don't ever doubt it." I slowly unfolded the worn paper. She could tell from my reaction that I didn't expect her to have kept it for so long. "Do you know why it's so worn out?" she asked. "I've read it countless times throughout my high school years. Your words strengthened me and I hope mine will now strengthen you." When I opened the mailbox a couple days later I was touched to find a letter with a small note attached. "In case you forget."

May 13th

★

Act: Make a list of all the things you love about yourself; the things that make you uniquely you. Look at yourself in the mirror and read the list aloud. Always remember that you are beautiful.

Quote: "When virtues are pointed out first, flaws seem less insurmountable." ~Judith Martin

Reflection: A famous line in scripture states, "Love your neighbor like you love yourself." I say, loving your neighbor is easy. It's loving yourself that's difficult. Once you begin to love yourself, loving others is simple. Remember this: There is something uniquely special about each and every person, something which only he or she can bring into this world. Without you the puzzle is incomplete. So start opening your eyes and begin to see the beauty that lies right before you.

May 14th

Act: Buy a bouquet of flowers and anonymously leave it on the doorstep of a well-deserving mom.

Quote: "Only by giving are you able to receive more than you already have." ~Jim Rohn

Reflection: It's not necessarily the flowers that will uplift someone, but the knowledge that someone is thinking of them, even when they stop thinking of themselves. An anonymous gift at the right moment can soothe a broken heart, instill hope, and inspire change. We will never know when the right moment will be. After all we are all going through our own behind-the-scenes struggles; the likelihood is that today is that day. The petals will wilt, the flower will die, but the memory and feelings of gratitude will forever remain.

Act: Tell your parents or mentor how much you love them. Say thank you! Simple? Yes! But, they need to hear that more than you know.

Quote: "I like not only to be loved, but also to be told I am loved." ~George Eliot

Reflection: Ever wonder why it's said that a child will never love their parent as much as a parent loves their child? Simple—the more you give, the more you love the object you are giving to.

In a split second the focus of a new parent's life transfers from themselves, the way it's always been, to this little, fragile, beautiful baby.

Caring for it, feeding it, clothing it, housing it. Babies don't come equipped with an instruction manual. But day in and day out, choice after choice, parents do what they believe is the very best for you. Sure, mistakes are made—after all, we're all human. But the more they give, the deeper their love grows, perhaps even overshadowing the love for their own dreams, goals, and aspirations. You are everything and they couldn't be happier. To give without the feeling of sacrifice but solely from love. That is a parent.

May 16th

♥

Act: Place a heartwarming note for your child or a young person in your life saying "I love you" tucked somewhere in their lunch box or under their pillow.

Quote: "Enjoy the little things in life because one day you'll look back and realize that they were the big things." ~Kurt Vonnegut

Reflection: The small bits of kindness we spontaneously share with those we love most leave a deep imprint and impression because they come with no strings attached. Stop planning, preparing, and plotting the moments you assume will create meaning, and simply take action.

May 17th

Act: Running late? (It happens to the best of us.) Make a phone call or send an email to let someone know you won't be there on time.

Quote: "The bad news is, time flies. The good news is, you are the pilot!" ~Michael Altshuler

Reflection: By valuing the time of others, we become mindful of time in general. Recognizing that each moment brings with it new opportunities and new possibilities yet to be discovered, to be enjoyed, to be shared. Time is fleeting; readily given out and wasted without thought that it will ever run out, disappear, and vanish. But make no mistake, time is one of the most valuable gifts we've been given during our short stay on this planet. Let's show others that we value their time as much as we value our own.

Act: Unplug and save energy.

Quote: "Look deep into nature and you will understand everything." ~Albert Einstein

Reflection: Every year billions of kilowatt hours of electricity in homes are used by appliances that aren't on but are still consuming energy. Unplug your appliances and chargers when they aren't in use and you can begin making a dent in saving our planet.

May 19th

🍎

Act: Need a hand? Offer to help a teacher or classmate during your lunch break.

Quote: "I am only one, but I am one. I cannot do everything, but I can do something. And I will not let what I cannot do interfere with what I can do." ~Edward Everett Hale

Reflection: A helping hand is someone who reaches out at the exact moment when you're ready to call it quits, throw in the towel, and worst of all, begin questioning whether you were crazy to try. On those fateful days, a simple offer to help can make all the difference. The struggle still lies ahead, but a renewed sense of assurance clothes you and suddenly you have the strength to push forward.

Act: Sign up to read to the elderly at a local senior citizen home. You will both enjoy the gift of storytelling.

Quote: "A little kindness from person to person is better than a vast love for all humankind." ~Richard Dehmel

Reflection: The lessons and experiences we learn during our short time on this amazing planet are only as good as the people we can share them with. My weekly trip to the old-age home was one of those experiences that reminded me of this every time I went. What started out as an outing with a handful of students turned into something with lifelong meaning.

One of the men at the home had a love for history and a knack for telling stories. Each story had a lesson; something to be learned, something to reflect on. I for one could've sat there all day. His eyes were fixated on the students who looked up to him in admiration as he regaled them with story upon story. I stood at a distance and watched the magical connection form. I knew that it would be an experience the students would recall as they got older. They didn't realize the impact their visit had on him, and I often find myself wondering if he realized the impact he had on them.

This man has since passed, but the stories he shared, the memories he created, the nuggets of wisdom he instilled will remain forever.

Act: Give the right of way to a pedestrian.

Quote: "Good actions give strength to ourselves and inspire good actions in others." ~Plato

Reflection: Kindness is something we are all aware of but when we find ourselves in a rush or under pressure we often close an eye to what we know to be the kind thing to do.

It's precisely the moments we embrace kindness instead of pursuing our immediate needs that set us apart from the rest. Stay true to your heart and instead of honking your horn, let kindness guide you. Think of the ripple of possibilities that can emerge from being a bit more mindful.

May 22nd

Act: Give up your parking spot to someone else that's looking, even if you got there first. Unexpected kindness is always cherished and remembered.

Quote: "Kindness can open doors where doors were thought not to exist." ~Erica Wilson

Reflection: Sometimes we wake up and everything seems to unravel at the seams and when you think it can't get worse, it does. With only one more minute to find a spot and make your way to an important meeting, the one you can't be late to, you can't seem to find anything. Everyone is one step ahead of you that day as you continue to miss one spot after the next. This must be some kind of joke and you're today's specimen.

You shake your head as you see yet another lucky person find a spot that you were only ten seconds late to catching. But then the person hesitates and gives you the spot, seeming to say: "I've been seeing you circling. You seem nervous. Go right ahead, I'll get the next one."

Perhaps the day won't be as bad as you initially anticipated.

May 23rd

Act: Make a point to begin each phone call with a smile and a few kind words. Your smile can most certainly be heard and it makes all the difference to the person on the other end of the line.

Quote: "Smile with your lips, smile with your eyes, smile with your heart and your soul and your life." ~Terri Guillemets

Reflection: Life Vest Inside's event Dance for Kindness was less than a week away and with three hundred people registered to take part in the NYC event I still hadn't secured a rehearsal space. I must have walked into over twenty locations that day and with each passing "no" or "I'm sorry" my anxiety rose. As I passed by the New Victory Theater I decided to give it one last shot. The security guard informed me that the executive I was hoping to speak with was in a meeting, but he kindly transferred me to her assistant, Rhesa. We only spoke for a few moments, but I could hear the kindness in her voice. "I'll do what I can," she said.

In the end, we weren't able to secure the New Victory Theater, but luckily when I returned home that evening, I received a call from a local community member offering a space he had free of charge. I kept in touch with Rhesa via email, keeping her posted about the space, the event, and how phenomenal it all turned out.

Two weeks down the road we had both decided it was finally time for us to meet in person. Rhesa is now volunteering with Life Vest Inside. All from a friendly call.

Act: We all can benefit from a little affection. Give someone a hug. The kind that comes from the heart, not just the arms.

Quote: "There is no small act of kindness. Every compassionate act makes large the world." ~Mary Anne Radmacher

Reflection: Sometimes what we need more than anything is to be held for a few extra seconds. Did you know that hugs make you happier, healthier, more relaxed, and improve your relationships? Studies have shown that hugs decrease stress and boost happiness levels. A good hug is a quick fix to get oxytocin flowing in your body. Oxytocin, the cuddle hormone, promotes social bonding, exerts an immediate calming effect, increases trust and generosity, strengthens the immune system, and boosts virility. It's no wonder that studies have shown that couples who hug more are more likely to stay together. There's only one catch: It has to be a good, twenty-second hug to qualify. So get your stopwatch ready and start giving out free hugs!

May 25th

★

Act: Your brain needs exercise just as much as your body. Segment a few minutes each day to read the book you've been hoping to make time for. It won't move from your shelf unless you make a conscious effort to begin.

Quote: "You will never find time for anything. If you want time you have to make it." ~Charles Buxton

Reflection: When things are important we have to make time instead of saying there is not enough time in the day. There will always be work, there will always be a long to-do list, there will always be another project, another place to go, another errand to run, another phone call to make. We have to consciously segment time for ourselves. Simply knowing that you're giving yourself a break will reenergize you and you'll return back to work with a greater appreciation and perhaps a better perspective.

Act: Stay humble and be true to yourself. Greatness does not depend on what others think of you, but what you think of yourself.

Quote: "Being humble means recognizing that we are not on earth to see how important we can become, but to see how much difference we can make in the lives of others." ~Gordon B. Hinckley

Reflection: Confidence and arrogance look the same, but are diametrically opposed. One springs from a true sense of self-value, the other is steeped in self-loathing and insecurity. One with a yearning to unite and empower, the other with an insatiable thirst for honor. One leading to a life of serenity, the other a life of frustration. One instilling love and acceptance, the other feeding off of fear and intimidation.

True confidence stems from the most prized character trait—humility.

The challenge isn't to attain humility, but to keep it in spite of the wins, the successes, and the praise. Whereas genuine humility increases in proportion to a humble person's success, arrogance graciously crowns itself preemptively, taking pride in every triumph and casting a shadow on others.

The confident and humble see all people in the same light, recognizing that no individual is superior to another and that all deserve to be lifted up.

May 27th

🏠

Act: Prepare a nice home-cooked meal for your family or roommate. Always cooking the meals? Make a night of it and get the rest of the members of your household involved.

Quote: "If love is the treasure, laughter is the key." ~Yakov Smirnoff

Reflection: All the parents headed off on a trip with my grandparents for two weeks and it was just us cousins. Friday was rapidly approaching and the question on all of our minds was, who's cooking Shabbat dinner? Coming from traditional Jewish homes, our moms were always in the kitchen cooking up a storm; everything was always taken care of for us, so what did we do now? It was another opportunity for a great adventure! Through a ridiculous amount of texting back and forth we finally decided we would cook the meal together. Checklists were made, ingredients were bought, and we all met up at my aunt's house. Now all that was left was to actually cook, but of course none of us had the slightest clue what we were doing. It didn't turn out to be the best-tasting meal, but it was the most memorable. Together, laughing, smiling—what could be better!

Act: Pay respects to someone who has lost a loved one. Let them know that they can count on you as a friend in both the good times and the bad.

Quote: "We are not here on earth to see through each other, we are here to see each other through." ~Gloria Vanderbilt

Reflection: When my Grampsi passed away, I shut down. How could I envision embarking on the rest of the journey of life without our steadfast captain at the helm steering our ship forward, protecting us from the storm that only a well-trained captain could see? Droves of people passed in and out offering their condolences, but I couldn't see them, I couldn't even hear them. The first day I attempted to head back to work, my co-worker sat by my side on the carpet of my office floor, and held me while I cried. I didn't see her, I didn't hear her, but I felt her and in that moment it was all I needed to find my way back.

May 29th

Act: Practice understanding. Assume the best in others.

Quote: "Our days are happier when we give people a bit of our heart rather than a piece of our mind." ~Ritu Ghatourey

Reflection: Life has a tendency to throw curveballs our way. No matter how well we may think we have things planned, we can never account for the unexpected bumps in the road. We may cringe when those encounters take us by surprise, but we keep moving on, keep pushing forward, making the best of the hand we've been dealt. The choice is always ours. You can allow frustration, anger, and hopelessness to sink its paws into the recesses of your mind. Or, you can take a step back to realize and understand that life doesn't come with a set of rules that we can easily follow, but rather it moves at its own pace without regard of the endless preparation we've poured into it. By understanding the ups and downs of life, the occasional loops and spins, the unexpected hurdles, we can begin to grasp that the challenges we face aren't ours to face alone.

Each person has their own battles, their own struggles, their own plans foiled, and hopes unrealized. Let's see ourselves in one another and suddenly we can readily and more easily empathize when the day doesn't seem to go precisely as we planned. You'll find that the more willing and accustomed you are to give others the benefit of the doubt, the more likely you are to receive it in return.

May 30th

❦

Act: Take a walk. Give yourself the time to take in the beauty and appreciate nature.

Quote: "In every walk with nature one receives far more than he seeks." ~John Muir

Reflection: Beauty is often found in the silence, in the stillness, in the calm. It is found in the moments in which we have the courage and tenacity to step away from the noise, the hustle and bustle, and the never-ending race to a finish line that doesn't exist.

Listen to the birds sing, the leaves dance, and cast your eyes on the amazing combination of colors, sounds, fragrances, and sights found right outside your window. They're all speaking to you. It's time to listen.

May 31st

Act: Try and settle a fight between friends. Kind words and patience can solve any problem.

Quote: "Peace is not the absence of conflict, but the ability to cope with it." ~Dorothy Thomas

Reflection: Peace is something that ought to be pursued in spite of how cunning it may be in escaping us. What is peace but the acknowledgment of beauty and significance in another in spite of the obvious and apparent differences that exist? Like a forest fire, our words can escalate a feud and transform it into an all-consuming blaze. But with the proper intention and sensitivity, our words can quell even the greatest flame. Resolve to be a lifelong pursuer of peace, remembering that the immense joy in helping two people catch a glimpse of the view from the other side is far more intriguing than the sudden excitement of being the "innocent" witness and bystander to controversy.

June 1st

🌍

Act: Offer a cup of coffee or bottle of water to your local delivery-eryman. What a great way to keep them energized and remind them that their service hasn't gone unnoticed.

Quote: "Great opportunities to help others seldom come, but small ones surround us every day." ~Sally Koch

Reflection: We need not travel far and wide, amass great fortune, attain success, acquire awards and medals, or be an acclaimed celebrity to leave our mark. Rather, the mark we leave on this world is attributed to the lives of the people we touch. We simply need to open our door, open our heart, and see. See the people standing before us, the people we cross as we go about our day-to-day activities and seize the small opportunities to remind others that their presence is felt.

If making someone's day simply takes a small gesture, I say why not?

As I handed the deliveryman a bottle of water and snack bar on one hot summer day, it was clear he wasn't often greeted with kindness. Part of me was touched, the other disappointed. Somewhere along the way kindness became something foreign, something unexpected, something that shocks people and takes them by surprise.

His show of gratitude warmed my heart, but I long for the day when the shock factor is gone and all that remains is the warmth.

Act: Getting gas? Leave an extra $10 at the pump for the next person coming to fill up. What a wonderful surprise that would be.

Quote: "No act of kindness, no matter how small, is ever wasted." ~Aesop

Reflection: With an empty tank and an empty wallet I pulled up to a gas station. I sifted through a thin wallet I leave in my car which usually carries several bucks in case of emergencies, and this was definitely an emergency. The tank was empty, and the wallet was empty. In a fit of panic I began presenting my case to the gas attendant. "I'm trustworthy. I'll rush right back to pay you." He smiled at me, filled the car with $10 of gas, and waved me forward to head out. I thanked him profusely and told him I would be back right away. He shook his head, smiled, and said, "Don't worry about it." He called over one of the other attendants and they excitedly shared their story. "Last week a gentleman filled up his car. Before pulling away he handed us an extra $10 on top of a generous tip. We asked him what it was for. He smiled and said that one day someone with an empty tank will find their way to this gas station, but they won't have any money on them. This $10 is earmarked for that person on that very day. We had no clue when or if an opportunity would present itself, and here you are just a week later."

We don't always see the impact our kindness has, but rest assured each of us leaves an imprint on this world deeper and more meaningful than we can ever imagine.

June 3rd

Act: Say "hello" to people you do not know. Sure, you may get a few confused looks, but you'll also get some smiles and positive energy flowing back at you.

Quote: "Let your heart guide you. It whispers, so listen carefully." *~The Land Before Time*

Reflection: My friend Rosie could have stuck to simply doing her laundry, but where was the fun in that? She sat between two women who were each engrossed in their own activities. She struck up a simple conversation that turned into an afternoon of bonding and camaraderie.

The three conversed, jumping from topic to topic covering everything from the news, the weather, holidays, and politics. Both women had family members serving in the Army, and once they got on this topic the conversation deepened.

The laundry cycle was long over, but there they sat conversing, sharing, connecting. It turns out they had more in common than they initially anticipated. Rosie frequently sponsored soldiers, sending them care packages and letters in recognition of their service. When hearing that one of the woman's grandsons has received little to no support from his family, Rosie offered to send him a letter and one of her care packages.

A simple hello, an empathetic ear, and a compassionate heart transformed a mundane visit to the Laundromat into an incredible friendship.

June 4th

✿

Act: Be a team player at work. The simple knowledge that someone has your back makes you feel more confident as you head into work.

Quote: "A man without comrades is like the left without the right." ~Solomon ibn Gabirol

Reflection: Being a team player is the recognition and understanding that we are all in this together and that someone doesn't always have to fail for another to succeed. Acknowledge the value you bring to the table and suddenly your entire vision becomes altered.

We are all instruments playing the same symphony, but if we fail to listen to the other instruments as we play along to the notes, the music fades and all you're left with is noise. Open your eyes, open your heart, and become the team player you were meant to be.

June 5th

Act: Waiting to be seated at a busy restaurant? Offer to switch spots with the family or couple behind you. You'll never remember the few extra minutes you waited to be seated, but you'll always remember the smiles on their faces.

Quote: "A fellow who does things that count doesn't usually stop to count them." ~Albert Einstein

Reflection: After a quarrel with her boyfriend, PeiLin found herself emotionally drained, and nothing cures an aching heart more than a nice hearty meal. She sat down at a restaurant, ordered to her heart's content, and began digging in. Moments later, in walked a family of seven. The only large table was right beside hers, but it only sat four.

She could've finished her meal, could've excused her lack of action on a broken heart, but it was precisely the action of giving that carries with it the greatest level of comfort and she knew that. Without a moment's hesitation, she suggested to the waiter to move her to another table so there would be ample room for the family. The waiter was in shock, but it was clear that he was extremely grateful.

Whether the family remembers her gracious offer or not, the moment continues to fill PeiLin with joy every time she dines out.

June 6th

✦

Act: Go to sleep earlier than usual, give your body and mind the extra rest they deserve. Tomorrow is another day.

Quote: "Rest and self-care are so important. When you take time to replenish your spirit, it allows you to serve others from the overflow." ~Eleanor Brown

Reflection: There's an old story of a king whose servant had but one task, to fill the king's cup with water each day and bring it to him. The servant was very careless and would often drop the cup, scratching it and putting holes in its sides. Soon enough the cup had so many holes that by the time the servant brought it to the king there was no water to be found. The contents of it simply poured onto the ground. Our body is that cup, a vessel, with which we have the ability to do and accomplish great feats. It's the most precious object given to us. But if we don't care for it and allow it to repair itself during a great night's sleep, we'll damage its outer shell so badly that no amount of water will help it fulfill its ultimate purpose. Treat your body with love and you will feel the improvement more than just physically.

Act: Lend your skills, talents, and experience to someone free of charge.

Quote: "Successful people are always looking for opportunities to help others. Unsuccessful people are always asking, 'What's in it for me?'" ~Brian Tracy

Reflection: I've always had a fascination with puzzles. An assortment of pieces each with a different shape, different color, but every single one the same size. Each piece having its specific place and purpose, a specific meaning to the entirety of the puzzle and the beautiful picture it's part of.

There's no room for arrogance; one piece boasting that it has a far more superior role than another. No fear that another piece's shape or splash of color will outshine the most bland and inconspicuous piece. No fear that another piece can sabotage you and take your place. In place of fear, in place of arrogance, there lies an unspoken confidence. A confidence that each piece will eventually find its place.

There's a unanimous understanding that by lending an adjacent piece a part of your essence, a bit of your color, a sliver in your arena, it will simply enhance the beauty of both pieces.

Share and share wholeheartedly.

Rest assured that when we give, our essence isn't diminished, it shines brighter.

Act: "How was your day?" Such simple words with such a powerful meaning. Take the time to ask your family how their day has gone. Here's the important part—really listen.

Quote: "Love is a fruit in season at all times, and within the reach of every hand." ~Mother Teresa

Reflection: "How's everything?" "How are you doing today?" "How are you feeling?" We ask these questions all the time, but how often do we wait to hear the answers? It has become an accepted practice to inquire how someone is doing, but very rarely do we engage past the question. Be mindful to pause, listen to the response, and reply. Perhaps that someone is really in need of a listening ear. If we don't slow down enough, we could miss that amazing opportunity. To be there for another is a privilege; let's take advantage of it to the fullest!

As a kid, I had a tough time trusting that people truly cared. I remember countless times feeling alone, down, or worried when the question was posed, "How are you?" I'd respond, "Everything's great!" But in my heart, I hoped and wished that they would ask once more. When they would walk away it was just further proof that people didn't truly care. Be mindful of looking into someone's eyes when you ask them how they're doing or how their day was. You'll see right away if there is something they would like to share with you. They just may need an extra moment to feel comfortable to open up.

June 9th

♥

Act: Call one of your siblings and plan a fun evening out to catch up. Only child? Reach out to a cousin or old friend. The older we get the more we need and can appreciate those who knew us when we were younger.

Quote: "A man travels the world over in search of what he needs, and returns home to find it." ~George Moore

Reflection: Friends come and go but family lasts a lifetime. Sure, there have been rough patches, flashes of anger when you promised that you'd never forgive them, never speak to them. But at the end of the day, know that they will be by your side during your darkest times and when you finally make your way to the other side.

June 10th

☀

Act: Give a waiter a generously big tip before your meal. TIPS = To Insure Proper Service.

Quote: "If there be any truer measure of a man than by what he does, it must be by what he gives." ~Robert South

Guest Reflection: It was 3:00 am and I couldn't sleep. I hadn't eaten much all day and was starving. I found myself in an all-night diner hoping to fill my stomach. When the server approached my table, she looked tired. I asked how she was doing and she curtly responded, "It's 3:00 am and I'm working, how do you think I'm doing? What do you want to drink?" I placed my order for an iced tea and she quickly went off to grab it.

When she returned, I handed her a $10 bill. She asked me what it was for. I said it was her tip. She was speechless for a moment, and I noticed her eyes begin to tear up.

As she tended to the other tables, I noticed that she seemed to have a bit more bounce in her step, and a smile on her face the rest of the time I was there. Before I left, she insisted on a hug, which I happily gave. She didn't notice the additional $5 I left her. Sure, I could have responded to her crude remark with my very own condescending comeback and felt completely justified in doing so. But what would that have accomplished? I made the choice to rise above and lift her with me. It made a world of difference for the both of us and I headed out of the diner that evening with a full stomach and a nourished soul. ~Jeff Kuske

June 11th

🌱

Act: Sign a petition in support of our planet.

Quote: "It is in the shelter of each other that people survive."
~Irish Proverb

Reflection: Your voice matters, you just need to believe it! Everything is made up of potential energy. How we use it determines its worth, its value, and its impact.

We may not always see the direct payoff of our involvement, time, and energy. But giving with a pure heart is giving without expectation of reward. Recognizing that simply being a piece of the puzzle, even unnoticed, is reward in and of itself.

June 12th

🍎

Act: Share some wisdom. Help someone prepare for a test. You'll be surprised by how much you end up learning while you're at it.

Quote: "You give but little when you give of your possessions. It is when you give of yourself that you truly give." ~Kahlil Gibran

Reflection: There's no greater gift than bestowing knowledge; not mere facts and figures but the ability to take a seemingly complex and convoluted idea, break it down to its parts, look into the eyes of a person who has had such a hard time grasping it, and suddenly watch it miraculously click! The moment when the information taught isn't just being memorized, but understood. And you are left with the great gift of knowing that information doesn't stop with itself, but can be applied to endless problems. Knowledge is power, but shared knowledge is the freedom to use that power.

June 13th

🌐

Act: Grab some sidewalk chalk and create an inspiration pathway down your block. There is always someone in need of a bit of inspiration.

Quote: "Some people want it to happen, some wish it would happen, others make it happen." ~Michael Jordan

Reflection: In the summer of 2010, I received a call from some of my former students. "We miss you! Let's hang out; we need some good Orly time." I jumped in the car, picked them up, and headed out to have some fun. Facing the obstacles of high school drama had taken its toll on their self-esteem and they were in need of a confidence boost. The car ride was filled with words of encouragement and a very clear message: "Believe in yourself."

We parked the car and headed out when one girl stopped in her tracks. "Orly, do you see this?" Along the expanse of the sidewalk written in sidewalk chalk were some of the very same empowering phrases uttered during our car ride. The biggest of them all—BELIEVE IN YOURSELF." I'm a firm believer that everything happens for a reason. "This is it!" I declared. I had been tirelessly searching for a location to shoot my film, *Kindness Boomerang,* and in that instant I realized it was right there in front of me. *Kindness Boomerang* was shot along that same walkway and the positive energy used to write those powerful phrases found their way into the essence of the film. To the anonymous artist who decorated the sidewalk with gems of hope and inspiration—thank you!

Act: Witness an accident? Call the authorities to let them know. Don't assume someone else dialed 911—they may be assuming the very same thing.

Quote: "One kind action leads to another. Good example is followed." ~Amelia Earhart

Reflection: It's our inability to realize that we matter that allows us to easily assume our actions or inactions don't make much of a difference. Does your voice matter? That depends on whether you utilize it. Peoples' assumption that their vote doesn't count, that their involvement is unimportant, is the same reason they assume their kindness will go unnoticed. "I'm sure someone else called." "I'm sure he has someone he can speak to." "I'm sure someone else said thank you." "I'm sure someone else . . ." Embrace the power of you. Perhaps someone else did, but what if they didn't?

June 15th

Act: Offer your seat on the bus or train to someone carrying heavy packages. Sure, we may be tired as well, but I can assure you that such an act of kindness will rejuvenate you.

Quote: "To give and then not feel that one has given is the very best of all ways of giving." ~Max Beerbohm

Reflection: Positive energy magically flows from one person to the next leaving a trail of smiles in its path. As I hopped onto the train at rush hour with a friend we were shocked and excited to find an open seat. We went back and forth for a few seconds debating who would take the vacant seat. He insisted and I gladly sat down knowing that within minutes I would find the opportunity to gift the seat forward to someone who needed it more than I did. It only took a few seconds before I gladly offered the seat to an older woman. She sat down, smiled, and was grateful to rest her legs. And so the kindness train began. Moments later a mom walked onto the train with her two children. It was clear it was a hectic day for her. Without hesitation the woman stood up to offer the mom a place to sit. Seeing this, the young man sitting next to her got up and insisted the older woman take a seat back down. Luckily I always carry Catching Kindness cards in my pocket. As I handed them out, a conversation began.

The weight of the day was lifted and an air of kindness and positivity filled our little section of the train.

✿✿

Act: Leave a positive recommendation for someone you work with on LinkedIn.

Quote: "When we seek to discover the best in others, we somehow bring out the best in ourselves." ~William Arthur Ward

Reflection: Giving a person recognition for what they've done gives them even greater incentive to continue putting their best foot forward.

You open your inbox and there it is, a request for a recommendation. You have two options: mark it as unread, adding it to the long list of things you will take care of in some magical, imaginary day that never seems to come, or take the next three minutes to type a heartfelt recommendation for someone who may have given of themselves to further your cause, your business, or your professional life.

When the work is done we tend to forget the people who got us there. It may no longer be a priority for you, but you never know how much of an impact those three minutes may have in securing a future job for that person. Don't assume to know whether something is or is not important for an individual at that exact moment; imagine yourself in their shoes and suddenly three minutes is no longer a sacrifice, it's an opportunity.

Act: Frame a picture that captures a beautiful moment you shared with a family member or friend and ship it to them.

Quote: "Taking pictures is savoring life intensely, every hundredth of a second." ~Marc Riboud

Reflection: Pictures have a magical way of transporting us back to a memory.

When my great aunt Taunt Vanda was diagnosed with Alzheimer's a piece of my heart shattered. I couldn't accept the fact that she would no longer be able to recall all the memories we shared. When my house burnt down it took with it loads of childhood memories, not to mention thousands upon thousands of pictures. Sifting through some of the photos that miraculously survived I found my favorite picture of the two of us from back in the day. I remember crying when I found it. It was time to face my fear and visit her, but I wouldn't be going empty-handed. Handing her the framed picture, I looked into her eyes and began singing what I remember of the Enrico Macias song we once sang together in unison. She couldn't speak much, but then again we never needed to communicate with words to understand one another. Perhaps everyone thought I was just being hopeful, but as her hands stroked the picture and she pointed to my face I knew that even though the memories had faded in her mind, they would always remain very much alive in her heart and in mine.

June 18th

⭐

Act: Practice saying the words "I'm sorry" when you're wrong. Apologizing isn't always the easiest thing to do, especially when it comes to family, but it is an extremely freeing experience.

Quote: "We can easily forgive a child who is afraid of the dark; the real tragedy of life is when adults are afraid of the light." ~Plato

Reflection: Admitting our mistakes and our errors in judgment are extremely vital in our efforts to building a kinder world. If we can readily admit that we make mistakes and that those mistakes don't define us, our perspective about the mistakes of others changes drastically. We are all human beings with intentions to do our best, but sometimes things don't turn out as we had planned. Perhaps apologizing will make it easier to accept the apologies of others.

Act: Treat a couple or someone sitting alone at dinner to a dessert on you.

Quote: "Never get tired of doing little things for others. For sometimes, those little things occupy the biggest part of their heart." ~Ida Azhari

Reflection: As my friend Jeff sat down for lunch he spotted an older couple from the corner of his eye. They were having a tense conversation throughout the course of their meal. He didn't pay heed to what they were ordering or to the spoken and unspoken words between them. He simply saw the pain in their eyes and the sadness in their hearts. Some time passed, they finished their meal, waved over their server, but to the older man's surprise the bill had been paid and a kindness card had been left behind. "You've been tagged by the Random Acts of Kindness club. Pay it forward . . . and have a great day!" The man looked at the receipt and the card in disbelief. "Is this a joke?" he asked the server. "No joke, sir, your bill has been paid in full." Still in disbelief, he looked back down at the paid bill, the card, smiled at his wife, and suddenly the tension melted away. With the bill lifted in the air, he stood up and addressed the restaurant. "I don't know who did this, but thank you. Thank you! I will most certainly pay it forward." With that, the couple left the restaurant a bit happier, a bit calmer, and a bit more grateful to be alive. Jeff knew he just got a great bargain. The smile on his face and the warmth in his heart was worth more than any lunch bill.

🏠

Act: Start a family WhatsApp group to keep in touch and stay connected! Warning: You may need to silence your Whats-App notifications.

Quote: "A happy family is but an earlier heaven." ~George Bernard Shaw

Reflection: When my grandpa passed away we all took it very hard. He was everything to my family and we were as close as we were because of the values he instilled in us. The fear of what would happen crept into all of our minds. Would his loss be the breakdown of our family's connectedness?

We've never been much of a tech family, that's for sure, but one cousin decided to create a WhatsApp group—"Grampsi's Legacy." All of his children, sons-in-law, grandkids, and his eldest great-grandkids connected in one chat. It started off as a place to share stories, funny selfies, and tons and tons of newborn baby pictures and grew into a place where our love, respect, and appreciation for what our Grampsi left us continues to grow.

After a long day of work, I glance at my phone to see 268 unread WhatsApp messages. I can't wait to read all of them.

Act: Start a gym routine with a friend. A healthy choice and a fun bonding experience all wrapped up in one. We all need a bit of a nudge to get us there. I know I do!

Quote: "Few things in the world are more powerful than a positive push." ~Richard M. DeVos

Reflection: With each passing day we tell ourselves, "Tomorrow is a new day. I'll start then." But the longer something remains on our to-do list, the less likely we are to ever check it off. Interestingly, it becomes our token item reminding us that the work is never done which allows us to justify why we haven't managed to get to it just yet. Doing a quick assessment of our "to-do list never done," we may find that the tasks remaining are the things that benefit ourselves.

Often people misconstrue kindness as an act performed solely for others, removing themselves from the equation. But with a closer look we'll find that kindness for oneself is just as vital as kindness for others. Remember, our body is our most important vessel. Without it we lose the capability to perform all of those wondrous acts of giving that we hold in such high regard. So take good care and let's do away with the laziness that justifies our inaction. You can do it. You know you can. It all begins with the first step.

June 22nd

Act: Deciding whether to call or text? When in doubt, make the call! It's more personal, plus it has the added bonus of establishing a clear line of communication.

Quote: "The single biggest problem in communication is the illusion that it has taken place." ~George Bernard Shaw

Reflection: In this age of technology we have so many options to communicate with those in our lives. It's a wonder how we got along without the gadgets and gizmos that appear to make our lives easier. We have access to people all over the world at the press of a button, yet there seems to be something missing.

The human voice is an amazing thing. The tone, the cadence, the volume can all send a greater message than the words themselves. A voice at the other end of the phone becomes much more personal and meaningful than a simple text or email. Texts serve a purpose, but so much gets lost and they are often the source of misunderstanding.

June 23rd

✦

Act: Pick up a bouquet of flowers to decorate your house.

Quote: "Be somebody who makes everyone feel like a somebody." ~Robby Novak

Reflection: During my years teaching, every Friday, without fail, a bunch of students piled into my car as we headed out on our very own Kindness Journey. Stop #1: With hearts filled with love, ears ready to listen, and hands carrying the most delicious bread, we headed into the old-age home to pay a visit to men and women who had become our mentors. The memories, friendships, and lessons we learned on those Friday excursions will forever be embedded in my heart and mind. Stop #2: 7-Eleven to load up on some treats. As we headed to Stop #3, the flower shop, we'd discuss some of the things we learned, always keeping in mind a core lesson that was stressed in both my car and my classroom: Kindness begins at home! It started off as an errand I ran, picking out flowers for my mom on Friday. Naturally they would join me and eventually they too began picking out flowers for their moms. It became one of the highlights of our journey, watching them contemplate the best arrangement that would bring an extra smile to their moms' faces. I knew that regardless of which flowers they chose their moms would be ecstatic, but the extra special care they took to select the freshest-looking flowers made a simple action that much more unique. And, of course, a bouquet of flowers is never complete without a heartfelt, handwritten note. The happiness those flowers brought is most certainly alive and well.

June 24th

🍎

Act: Don't mess! Pick up garbage lying around on the floor of your school.

Quote: "If your actions inspire others to dream more, learn more, do more, and become more, you are a leader." ~John Quincy Adams

Reflection: One piece of trash is the beginning of many more pieces to follow. Here's something to consider: Are you more likely or less likely to leave your trash behind in a clean atmosphere or dirty atmosphere? Be the one to set the trend!

June 25th

Act: Donate sports equipment to a local school team. Sports are important for the body and the mind.

Quote: "If you only keep adding little by little, it will soon become a big heap." ~Hesiod

Reflection: Only three seconds to go and the crowd's going wild. Making the winning shot, hitting the tie-breaking homer, scoring the game-winning touchdown. It's the dream of many. You're at the right place at exactly the right moment and for those few seconds everything falls into place with such perfect motion and symmetry. The roar of the crowd, the adrenaline rushing through your body, and the inexplicable feeling of belonging to something much greater than yourself. Being a part of a team has the ability to empower, to uplift, to unite a group of individuals, and to tap into a greatness you never knew you had.

As a shy kid with little confidence, sports were always an outlet for me. A place I went to when I questioned myself and the world around me. On the court everything made sense and for that moment I got to feel great.

Every child, every person deserves the chance to not simply play, but to shine. To know that with enough practice anything and everything is possible. I didn't know it back then but playing sports shaped the person I would become, the perseverance I would have, the tenacity to never give up, to never back down.

Every child should have the chance to live that dream.

June 26th

Act: Receive excellent service at a restaurant? Take a few moments to write a short review.

Quote: "As we express our gratitude, we must never forget that the highest appreciation is not to utter words, but to live by them." ~John F. Kennedy

Reflection: Why is it that we are so quick to leave negative feedback, but rarely do we run to leave a positive review? Recognition of great service is shown to have a more meaningful impact on a person than a few extra dollars left in their tip. So the next time you head out for dinner, end the night with a dash of kindness.

June 27th

Act: Prepare a meal for a homeless person. The extra bit of love and effort you put into making the meal will most certainly come through.

Quote: "Let the rays of your heart shine on all who pass by."
~Terri Guillemets

Guest Reflection: It was coming up on the Fourth of July weekend. A day to grill, light fireworks, and spend time with family and friends.

When I answered the phone, I had no idea word had spread about my cooking talents. The local church was known for their outreach with the homeless community in the area and wondered if I could donate some food to help feed the homeless. It was a no-brainer. I jumped on board and began putting my smoking skills to good use.

Thirty pounds of chicken and nine racks of rib in two days! From prep to delivery, the feeling was wonderful, knowing that I could do my part by giving something personal to people who had nothing.

That feeling was all I needed, but when I opened the mail to find a thank-you letter from the pastor and a package filled with dozens of handwritten notes expressing gratitude I was beside myself. "Normally people don't care about us. You gave us food from your heart. You gave us love," the note read. ~Jeff Kuske

✿

Act: Offer a coworker a ride home or a lift to work.

Quote: "All I'm saying is, kindness don't have no boundaries."
~*The Help,* by Kathryn Stockett

Reflection: My student Sylvia and I had our commute to school timed to six minutes. To us those six minutes set the tone for the rest of the day, ensuring that regardless of how hectic life gets the day started with a smile. Getting to school on time was the only way Sylvia would escape the constant detention slips. She only lived a couple blocks away from me. I offered to drive her to school one week and before I knew it, one week turned into a daily routine we both looked forward to.

Each morning started with a song that would empower us to find the beauty in the world, the beauty in ourselves, and the beauty in the ordinary. We were both not great with lyrics so we started a game. Every few weeks one of us would choose a song, print the lyrics, and our morning drives became filled with laughter and music as we attempted to memorize the words. Some days one of us would enter the car on a low note, worried about a personal struggle we were facing, anxious about the future, but by the time we got to school we were smiling again, the song keeping us going all day.

The time we spend getting from one place to another is often misconstrued as waste, but with a little creativity you can fill those moments with some good old connecting. A great friendship may just be a short car ride away.

June 29th

🦋

Act: Give someone a heartfelt compliment today. It's simple, yet powerful. You just might make their day!

Quote: "Kindness is the one commodity of which you should spend more than you earn." ~T. N. Tiemeyer

Reflection: Being a mother of three, Ann didn't have much time to pay attention to her wardrobe or how she looked, but one thing was certain—she and her daughter were as happy as could be as they roamed about the pharmacy section of Target singing, "You are my sunshine." An unexpected compliment from a stranger turned this rather ordinary moment into a lasting memory of singing with her daughter and feeling grateful to be a mom. The stranger stopped them to say, "I need to tell you how very beautiful you are."

The idea of being beautiful at such a moment caught Ann off guard. After all she didn't feel particularly beautiful on that day; bedraggled, trolling around without a stitch of makeup, still working on the baby weight.

As they continued singing their song, the gentleman's words resonated in her mind. She realized that a person could radiate the beauty of a moment and she resolved to acknowledge and appreciate that beauty within each person she would meet. It feels good to notice people, because it feels good to be noticed.

June 30th

✦

Act: Today focus on complimenting yourself and the things you love about you.

Quote: "Believe in yourself and all that you are. Know that there is something inside you that is greater than any obstacle." ~Christian D. Larson

Reflection: Seeing the beauty in ourselves allows us to more readily see the beauty in others. We all have our flaws, but sometimes great beauty can be seen within those flaws. Don't be so quick to judge yourself. Start practicing a bit more self-love for it will lead you to a love of others. Try seeing yourself through the eyes of someone who loves you.

July 1st

Act: Keep your cool! Even when the waves come crashing down, when your life seems to be unraveling at the seams, when the burden is too heavy to carry; stay calm, and take a deep breath. You can handle this.

Quote: "Life can only be understood backwards; but it must be lived forwards." ~Søren Kierkegaard

Reflection: When exhaustion, sadness, aggravation, shock, and confusion set in, peace of mind, perspective, and self-discipline disappear. Suddenly what was once right is now wrong, and what was once wrong now seems right. It's easy to get lost in the intensity of it all, but more rewarding to rise above in pursuit of something far more valuable—tranquillity.

A provocative remark can ignite anger, but even the most intense fury can be quelled with a gentle word. It serves as a true testament that strong people don't need aggressive words. While controlling anger requires great discipline and constant repetition, its rewards are endless.

Just as a surfer braces himself, caught off guard by an epic set rolling through, preparing his body and mind for what's to come, so too must we equip ourselves with the know-how to overcome anger when the unexpected blindsides us.

🏠

Act: Begin putting together a family tree. What a great way to learn more about your ancestors. Be creative and possibly gift it to your grandparents or another elderly family member.

Quote: "You must know where you came from yesterday, know where you are today, to know where you're going tomorrow." ~Trace A. DeMeyer

Reflection: "I've been wanting to do that for the longest time, but just never got around to it." Have you found yourself saying this at various points in your life? People often point to a lack of time as reason for not accomplishing the goals or following through on exciting things they had hopes of doing. Often it is simply the inability to break things down into its parts. Can you actually make a family tree in one day? Of course not! However, to make it come into being, as with everything else in life, you must take the first step. Pick up the phone and spend ten to fifteen minutes chatting with your parents, grandparents, aunts, or uncles to start backtracking some of that history. You just may find that another family member wants to join you on this great journey.

I can't recall a time when my grandpa looked as radiant and excited as he did when recounting with such fondness the memories hidden in the back of his mind after I dug deeper into his past. He'd been waiting for someone to help bring them to the foreground. Who would have thought a simple desire to create a family tree would spark a storehouse of family history that could have remained unveiled?

July 3rd

♥

Act: Take the time to help guide someone through a rough patch by drawing on your own past experiences.

Quote: "The only source of knowledge is experience." ~Albert Einstein

Reflection: Our experiences, both good and bad, are gifts of wisdom bestowed on us so that we may serve as their keeper until the time comes to pass them along to another in the form of advice. By drawing on our experiences to offer comfort and guidance to another we transform a simple experience into a life lesson that can save someone else untold stress and frustration. Be mindful that the intentions of your words stem from a place of gratitude, love, and genuine care for the other's well-being. Jealousy can often mask itself as advice and fool you into believing that your heart was in the right place. Outsmart jealousy by remembering that the world is filled with abundance and enough for each person's needs to be met. One person need not be down for another to rise. If you offer genuine, heartfelt advice, you've created a bond that will come back to help you when you need words of encouragement.

July 4th

Act: Out with friends or family for the Fourth? Make it a tech-free time and put away your cell phone.

Quote: "Do the right thing. It will gratify some people and astonish the rest." ~Mark Twain

Reflection: The world is hectic. Sometimes we become so reliant and tied to our electronic devices that even though they are supposed to keep us more connected to the world around us, ironically we feel less connected and more detached than ever. We constantly look at our phones or tablets to see what's going on around the world, but we often lose sight of the opportunity for human connection right in front of us.

Let's give the people in our lives the time and attention they most certainly deserve. You'll be surprised by how much more you learn from your surroundings and the people in them simply by looking a few degrees up. It's time to disconnect so we can connect more deeply.

July 5th

❧

Act: Get back to nature! Plan a hiking trip. Use the time to disconnect from the hustle and bustle of the city and reconnect with your very core.

Quote: "The secret powers of nature are generally discovered unsolicited." ~Hans Christian Andersen

Reflection: Nobody can deny the excitement of a city. The diversity of people, cultures, places to go, and attractions to see make them very popular, and rightfully so! This being said, cities tend to distract us from connecting with our roots, which are buried in nature. Planning a brief weekend trip to a campground or a hiking trail provides the perfect detox from city life. It doesn't matter whether an individual is flying solo or with friends and family, both scenarios provide deep healing.

Remaining open-minded and judgment-free allows us to experience nature's true gifts. Experimenting with mindful meditation can allow us to become aware of the sounds, scents, and sensations in a given area. This makes us conscious of things that previously went unnoticed. Walking barefoot provides us with the opportunity to tune into how our surroundings physically feel, while simultaneously connecting us with the earth's energy. Nature facilitates many activities that promote healing and relaxation. So grab a duffel bag, get outside, and allow nature to take its course.

July 6th

Act: Make a new friend. It's simple. Just introduce yourself to someone new. They won't bite.

Quote: "The easiest way to meet people is to just look like someone who is willing to listen." ~Robert Brault

Reflection: The more you recognize your inherent value the more likely you are to recognize the value in another person. Finding flaws and faults in others may be easier, but spotting their beauty and discovering the thing that makes them unique is far more rewarding. Dig a bit deeper.

July 7th

Act: Spend some time reading to kids at a children's hospital.

Quote: "Never put off until tomorrow what you can do today, because if you enjoy it today, you can do it again tomorrow."
~James A. Michener

Reflection: Reading is a great way to de-stress and immerse yourself in a new world, a world where the impossible is never out of reach. Go the extra mile and leave the children at the hospital with their very own writing kit, complete with a notebook, pencils, and maybe even a few creative writing prompts. It may very well be the ounce of encouragement they need to begin creating their very own story and forging a new chapter in their book of life. Remember, your very presence can have greater healing powers than any doctor-prescribed medicine.

Our time in this world may be limited but with every life we touch we etch our name and our legacy onto another page of someone's book and our impact remains forever.

July 8th

Act: Have a big lunch you can't quite finish? Pack it to go and look for an opportunity to share your meal with someone in need. Finished your meal? Buy an extra sandwich to gift forward to the homeless man you pass by each day. It's not about whether he accepts or declines, it's about the offer.

Quote: "Better to expose ourselves to ingratitude than fail in assisting the unfortunate." ~Du Cœur

Reflection: Famished, my friend Joey and I entered a restaurant not realizing that our eyes were bigger than our stomachs. After several bites we unexpectedly reached our limit. I don't remember much about the meal, but rather the conversation as we sat in the booth and began chatting about the power of kindness, the power of human interaction, and the power of giving forward without expectation of reward.

It was only three months into my work with Life Vest Inside, but Joey and I both knew the endless possibilities kindness could bring. As the waitress handed us the check, we looked at each other and knew we were thinking the same thing. "Can you pack this to go?" We spent the next ten minutes on a quest to find a homeless woman Joey saw each morning on his way to work. We finally found her sitting on a crate on the side of the road. Perhaps she had no material possessions but her heart and her eyes were filled to the brim with love as we handed her the sandwich, conversed for several minutes, and continued with our day. Her soul seemed to shine and that light penetrated our hearts. For me, that light has never faded.

July 9th

Act: Spread kindness through the power of your voice.

Quote: "The main thing is that you hear life's music everywhere. Most people hear only its dissonances." ~Theodor Fontane

Reflection: The eighth-grade trip to Washington, DC, was always one of the highlights of my students' final year in middle school. As a teacher, I loved seeing the kids connect with one another outside of school, break out of their comfort zone, and get to learn a bit more about themselves and others they may not normally interact with.

As we pulled into the mall, they were bursting with energy. We had been pumping them up for a big surprise excursion, and to be honest, I was just as excited as they were. Nothing beats a great scavenger hunt! We broke into teams and off we went with our list of tasks, like "Sing a song to someone and make them smile." Most of the teams were a bit intimidated by that task; not our team. We were up for the challenge. After all, being a little silly never hurt anyone. We were willing to put our egos aside for laughter. We spotted a mother and her child from a distance. Music can almost instantaneously uplift someone and make them feel the urge to jump to their feet and break into song and dance. We started to sing to them and one by one other people began joining in.

I can't remember who won or lost the scavenger hunt, but we most certainly raised the happiness factor in the mall that day.

July 10th

✿✿

Act: Start to see past the end of your nose. Greet the doorman, security guard, and maintenance staff with a smile.

Quote: "A smile is happiness you'll find right under your nose."
~Tom Wilson

Reflection: Taking a few moments to engage in conversation has the power to make people feel as important as they truly are! What are you waiting for? Break out of your shell because you can never go wrong with an extra bit of kindness. Will your greeting be reciprocated? Who knows. But on the off chance that your greeting may be the words of hope another person had been searching for, you'll find that the risk is more than justified.

Act: See someone who appears lost? Offer to give directions or provide assistance.

Quote: "Wherever there is a human being, there is an opportunity for a kindness." ~Lucius Annaeus Seneca

Guest Reflection: On a bus en route to Colombo, Sri Lanka, I found myself sitting a couple of seats away from an older lady. Unfortunately, she had no idea where in Colombo she was headed to or how to get to her final destination. Everyone could have remained within his or her own bubble, unaffected by the woman's troubles, but on that bus, on that day, something special happened.

One passenger after the next comforted her, reassuring her that she would get to where she needed to go. Within the two and a half hours it took to reach Colombo, a plan was hatched for some of the willing passengers to escort her to her destination. The rest of us chipped in and raised a considerable amount of money to ensure she was taken care of. The feeling of solidarity was overwhelming, inspiring, and humbling; a group of people who made a conscious decision to put their own plans on hold to help another. ~Chamith Wijayasekara

★

Act: Stop procrastinating! Schedule a checkup at the doctor or dentist. There will always be work, there will always be a long, never-ending to-do list, but your health comes first. Pick up the phone and make the appointment.

Quote: "Take care of your body. It's the only place you have to live." ~Jim Rohn

Reflection: Only once you make the decision that your health matters and that without it, nothing else does, will you begin to recognize the extreme importance of giving it a tune-up every so often. Why is it that only when we are in immense pain do we come to be grateful for the everyday simplicities.

I've never been a fan of going to doctors. It was only once my toothache had reached the point of excruciating pain that I finally made the effort to make a dentist appointment. What should have only taken an hour, a check-in every six months, ended up turning into an entire escapade that took me out of commission for several weeks. Things turned out okay, but had I addressed my toothache earlier it would've been a lot easier to fix. When we are in the midst of work, we fail to see the importance of the simple things. Let's take a proactive approach to our health as opposed to a reactive one.

Act: When faced with a choice, choose loyalty.

Quote: "Let loyalty and truth be paramount with you." ~Confucius

Reflection: Often we find ways of justifying the choices we make, but you know your heart. Remain loyal to your friend, family, customer, or employer; it pays off in the long run and the name you build for yourself will be one you can be proud of.

When I was first beginning my career as a teacher, I was a twenty-one-year-old woman with no real experience, just a passion to teach and a love for children. The Yeshivah of Flatbush took a chance on me anyway. When I walked into school on the first day of what would be the most transformative years of my life, I was trembling. It was just a temporary teaching position for only six weeks. I would never have expected those six weeks to turn into an offer to teach full-time for six more years.

When another school I had originally approached called me up offering an opportunity to teach at a much higher pay grade, I declined their offer. This may have come as a shock to them but it was a no-brainer for me. I was staying put; my loyalty was exactly where it needed to be.

The Yeshivah of Flatbush middle school took a chance on me at a time when I was afraid to take a chance on myself. No amount of money could replace that feeling. Some called me nuts, some called me naïve, some called me immature. I simply called it a choice.

July 14th

🏠

Act: Treat someone you live with to breakfast in bed.

Quote: "The way you help heal the world is you start with your own family." ~Mother Teresa

Reflection: The unexpected surprises in life are like the icing on a cake. The cake may taste great even without the icing, but oh boy, does it look more appetizing. Breakfast in bed is usually served on the side of "Happy Mother's Day!" "Happy Anniversary!" "Happy Birthday!" or "Happy Valentine's Day!"

Every day is a great day to let someone know how much you love them and it's often the thought we put into the unplanned moments that make a person feel truly loved and even more so, truly appreciated. Isn't it amazing what a little morning breakfast surprise can do for the person on the receiving end?

Act: Scroll through the contact list on your phone. Call or text the first person it stops at. Perhaps there's a reason you landed on their name.

Quote: "Sometimes, reaching out and taking someone's hand is the beginning of a journey." ~Vera Nazarian

Reflection: "Can you cast your vote for Life Vest Inside? Add your voice and we can win a $10K grant." I began scrolling down my contact list texting one person at a time hoping they may take a few seconds to show their support for the organization I'd started. I stopped and hesitated over one name in particular. The last text I had sent her didn't end off on a very positive note. Skip her name? If there was something wrong it was about time to clear the air. After all if someone responds with negativity, the likelihood is that there is a reason for it. I decided to respond with kindness, hoping for an opening to call and resolve what seemed to be a misunderstanding. Apparently an old wound stemming from a simple miscommunication was still open after five years and I never knew it. Five years may have passed, but it took five minutes to clear the air, save a friendship, and lay the groundwork for open and meaningful communication from that day forward.

July 16th

◉

Act: Think before you post. Give a second glance to a Facebook status or social media post that could potentially upset others before you post it.

Quote: "By swallowing evil words unsaid, no one has ever harmed his stomach." ~Winston Churchill

Reflection: A careless comment, look, or interaction can extract a knee-jerk reaction that we'll regret in hindsight. Tempers can flare and emotions can take hold of our rational thinking. It happens to the best of us. Combine irrational thinking, intense emotions, add the relative anonymity of social media, and it can be a powder keg ready to explode.

When someone angers you, frustrates you, or hurts you to your core, take a deep breath, let the initial feelings pass, and you'll magically see a way of putting a positive spin on something negative. The right words can make someone's day but the wrong ones can ruin a life. Choose to spread positivity.

July 17th

◆

Act: Adopt an attitude of gratitude for a day! Before biting into a juicy piece of fruit, take a moment. Look at the amazing creation you're holding in your hand.

Quote: "The whole secret of the study of nature lies in learning how to use one's eyes." ~George Sand

Reflection: Who would have thought that an ordinary orange would provide a sense of comfort to a room filled with uncertain and insecure high school students.

As I juggled an orange in the classroom, I realized the answer to their insecurities was in the palm of my hand. "Do any of you eat the orange for the peel?" A unanimous "no" followed.

"Really? Then what do you eat the orange for?"

"The fruit inside."

"Exactly."

The peel provides the fruit with the necessary protection to grow and develop, but its essence isn't its peel, it's what's underneath. The substance is inside. Comprised of individual sections each with a juicy filling and sweet taste. But what makes it even more amazing is that within this little tiny fruit exists the potential for it to become greater than itself: seeds. They are part of the continuous cycle, providing the capability for more fruit to be grown and more oranges to be made.

Peeling back the outer layer gives us the opportunity to unveil something far more valuable. Within every person lies the same potential, the essence of a person. But if we fail to look beyond the outer layer, we are bound to miss something truly beautiful. (In honor of Rabbi Miller, my beloved rabbi and mentor)

Act: Stick up for someone even if they aren't around. Now that's loyalty.

Quote: "A real friend is one who walks in when the rest of the world walks out." ~Walter Winchell

Reflection: We all strive to be an accepted part of a group. But how far will we go to achieve that? How far will we stray from the values we know to be right? In actuality, acceptance isn't given by a group of individuals. The first step of acceptance begins with you. To know yourself, to love yourself, and to accept yourself for who you are and what you represent, flaws and all. The moment we feel at one with who we are and proclaim what we stand for, the easier it is to love others. Once we're able to do that, sticking up for someone and remaining loyal no longer becomes a choice, but a way of life. It's never easy to be a leader, to stand up when everyone else is sitting down. Trust in your values, your instincts, your heart, and sure enough others will follow.

July 19th

Act: Invite your neighbors to dinner.

Quote: "If you have much, give of your wealth; if you have little, give of your heart." ~Rumi

Guest Reflection: It was a beautiful day to fire up my new smoker for the first time. Today happened to be my birthday, and friends came by to celebrate. I lived in an apartment complex at the time, but didn't know my neighbors at all. Truth be told, none of us had ever made an effort to get to know one another.

As the hours passed and the food slowly cooked, the air was filled with a delicious aroma. Throughout the day, I noticed the occasional neighbors walking by my apartment. Each time they would pause and glance at my smoker. My guests arrived and the food was ready. When my neighbors Zach and Michelle stepped outside to say hello I offered them a plate of food, which they gladly accepted.

It wasn't long before we were chatting and laughing as though we were old friends. What I didn't know was that Zach and Michelle recently managed to get themselves off the street, and slowly but surely have begun putting their lives back together. My friends and I embraced them into our circle, and a new and loving friendship was formed as we all gathered around to enjoy a meal. ~Jeff Kuske

July 20th

🐾

Act: Next time you pass by a lemonade stand—stop! Buy a cup of lemonade and make some yummy noises. Let the kids know how delicious it is.

Quote: "How beautiful a day can be, when kindness touches it." ~George Elliston

Reflection: The sun had barely begun to rise on that Sunday morning, but the house was filled with youthful excitement and the chatter of three children as they began assembling their very first lemonade stand. It wasn't until a couple hours in that they peered out the window to notice the thick clouds rolling in, spoiling their plans for a hot summer day in the sun selling their one-of-a-kind lemonade. But rain wouldn't get them down. They set up shop and searched in every direction, hoping, anticipating, and trusting that someone would slow down and give their lemonade a chance. Cars continued to fly on by and with each passing car, their hopes dwindled. Suddenly a car stopped, a young man got out, and spent a few minutes conversing with the kids. "No one is slowing down because of the rain, but we worked all morning on setting up the stand," they told him. He encouraged them to keep on going! "Don't you worry, keep your chin up and you just may be surprised." He drank his cup of lemonade and left. Less than five minutes later, the same young man pulled up. To their surprise he rolled down the back window of the car filled with five thirsty passengers anxious to try their lemonade. The children's smiles were priceless.

July 27st

Act: Offer a refreshment to a construction worker on a hot day.

Quote: "Open your heart—open it wide; someone is standing outside." ~Mary Engelbreit

Reflection: Construction is grueling work. It's exhausting, dangerous, and often unappreciated, yet without it we wouldn't have our roads, the stable architecture of our homes, or the intricate structure of our highways.

Many people fall under the misconception that kindness is a task or obligation, something to be done and checked off a list. Kindness is, in fact, a privilege. A special right and opportunity set aside for those bold enough, wise enough, and perceptive enough to see its immense value. Simply shifting our perspective changes everything.

We can practice it by simply acknowledging the hard work those around us do to keep our worlds turning.

July 22nd

✿

Act: Invite a coworker to join in on a group outing you have planned.

Quote: "Coming together is a beginning; keeping together is progress; working together is success." ~Henry Ford

Reflection: Sometimes we can get so wrapped up in our work, in the tasks, in the details that we lose sight of the big picture. We convince ourselves that we can't stop, that we have to keep pushing forward. But it's often within the breaks and unplanned interruptions that the most meaningful work gets done. The quality of work produced is only as good as the morale, motivation, and conviction of the people who produce it. Creating an environment of solidarity and friendship imbues work with meaning and passion.

Soon after starting Life Vest Inside, I was so busy and overworked that I could no longer decipher morning from evening. One day my intern came up to me and said, "Let's go! Turn off your computer; the work will be there tomorrow. You need to do something for you." I looked at her in confusion. "Where are we going?" I asked. "To a movie," she said, "and I won't take no for an answer." I couldn't believe she managed to pry me away from my desk but it was the best medicine I could've asked for. With that movie, I got a chance to take a step back and refresh, and come back to work with a renewed sense of purpose.

July 23rd

✤

Act: Invite someone shy to hang out with you and your friends. You may have more in common than you think.

Quote: "What lies behind you and what lies in front of you, pales in comparison to what lies inside of you." ~Ralph Waldo Emerson

Reflection: Humanity is best thought of as an orchestra. Each of us an instrument playing our part. Any seasoned musician will tell you that the power of an orchestra is not found within a single instrument or sound, but when those sounds come together to form a symphony. It's when we grant each instrument permission to shine together that those sounds become more than just noise, they form a song.

While some instruments play a barely detectable sound to accompany the symphony, their role is far from small. Every sound, every nuance elevates the music to a different level.

It is our responsibility as players, as fellow members of humanity, to strive to appreciate and highlight the subtleties of each other's notes while continuing to play our own. You may not simply discover a sound that was never heard before, you may give that sound a newfound voice so that others may hear it as well.

July 24th

⭐

Act: Drink more water. When you're healthy and energetic it is much easier to be kind.

Quote: "Thousands have lived without love, not one without water." ~W. H. Auden

Reflection: Water is truly the ultimate elixir of life. It represents healing, love, and compassion. Without water nothing grows or blossoms. Think about this—beneath the earth, beneath the ground lays the capability of birth. Life exists beneath the earth's surface, but without the rain the earth's potential is never realized. This is the same for humanity. When we feed ourselves water, we open ourselves up to become a conduit for allowing the amazing potential within us to come out and be shared into the world. You just may start getting more excited on rainy days. Realizing that what's falling from the sky isn't a day ruined, but a window of rebirth and regrowth sprouting. So, too, in life with its seemingly negative moments. When it seems like rain is pouring down on us and we can't figure out why, remember that rain and struggle give us life, and weathering rough times will benefit us tremendously in the long run.

July 25th

Act: Wheel your neighbor's trash can out for pick up.

Quote: "As we work to create light for others, we naturally light our own way." ~Mary Anne Radmacher

Reflection: The small gestures are the ones that lead to a life-long friendship. When Jeff moved into his current neighborhood, his neighbors Scott and Lisa were quick to make him feel at home. It began with an unexpected knock at the door and a tray of freshly baked brownies, but it flourished into a boomerang effect of kindness that lasted for years.

Scott and Lisa loved to travel and after returning home from one particularly long trip they had a curious feeling something had changed. Scott knocked on Jeff's door. "I know it down-poured during our time away, but it's as though the grass was freshly mowed. Do you know anything about that?" Jeff was a good poker player, the best. "Hmmm . . . I don't know anything about that." They caught up a bit and then headed back into their homes. Jeff smiled as he closed the door; his own mischievous way of repaying the couple for their generosity and hospitality. He thought he was in the clear, undetected and under the radar.

Three days had passed and he heard a familiar sound in his backyard. Outside on the lawn, Scott was mowing away.

July 26th

Act: Exercise more patience in your home. Even when things aren't going your way, even when you may be annoyed, keep calm and be polite.

Quote: "Courage is what it takes to stand up and speak; courage is also what it takes to sit down and listen." ~Winston Churchill

Reflection: Patience means keeping a sound mind. Start by recognizing that not everything goes as planned and those unplanned bumps in the road can more often than not become blessings in disguise. Take a deep breath and believe that everything will get done. We all have days when we're not on our game and all we hope for is someone to give us a bit of breathing room. Let's distribute some of that breathing room so there is more to go around.

Patience is life's constant test of character. Performing an act of kindness is an accomplishment, embodying it is a triumph.

July 27th

♥

Act: Invite a loved one on a day trip to somewhere new and exciting. Traveling, even locally, can awaken our spirits and imagination.

Quote: "Wherever you go, go with all your heart." ~Confucius

Reflection: New surroundings bring with them new perspectives, new creativity, new opportunity, and a renewed sense of self. Pulling ourselves away from our daily routine to bask in the light of the unknown and unexplained is an exercise that should be practiced by each and every person. You never know where inspiration may find you. You'll be surprised to discover that when you allow your mind to wander, wondrous things can happen. We all have deadlines, we all experience pressure, and we all use the excuse that we can't take a break to get away. But let us ask ourselves, if we're too busy to enjoy life and the people we love, what is all the rushing for?

◉

Act: Cheer on a teammate! Why not remind one another that each person is a vital part of the team.

Quote: "Encouragement is the fuel on which hope runs." ~Zig Ziglar

Reflection: Encouragement goes a long way. Inadequacy is a feeling that creeps up on every person at one point or another; the feeling that we don't have what it takes, that we fall short, that we let people down when they're counting on us to pull through.

The more we feed into our supposed shortcomings, the more they prove themselves to be true. Success is a state of mind; it's rooted in a person's willingness to own that success.

I will always remember the tension as the clock ran down in my community basketball semifinals game. Our team was the underdog with the worst record of the season, but we had heart and we pulled through in spite of what the record books showed. We wanted it bad, and we knew we could do it if we came together. Jenny, my teammate, stepped up to the foul line with less than ten seconds to go, down by one. She dreaded this moment, always telling herself that she could never make her foul shots. I looked her in the eye, took a deep breath, and said, "You can do it! You just need to believe it. Time to let go of the doubts and own this." She dribbled the ball, looked at the basket, and looked back again at me. I smiled and nodded my head, not taking my eyes off of her even after the ball left her hands; I knew she would make it. The following week we were headed to the championship; it was a game we'll never forget.

July 29th

⬥

Act: Gather a few friends and plant a flower garden in a place that the entire neighborhood can enjoy.

Quote: "There is not one blade of grass, there is no color in this world that is not intended to make us rejoice." ~John Calvin

Reflection: Perhaps growing up in a tiny mountain village in Germany sparked my friend's father's passion and genuine love for nature. But it wasn't simply nature, it was nature's impact; the smiles that naturally sprung on the faces of people, young and old, as they'd walk by a patch of radiant daffodils.

Moving to Brighton, he missed the wild flowers. The trees were bare, as were the expressions on those who would pass by them each day. He began planting daffodils under a single tree and smiled as he watched the glowing expressions on the faces of the neighborhood children as they stopped to show their parents.

He woke up one morning to find that the city council dumped mulch on the single tree with flowers underneath it. Apparently all the trees needed to look the same. He could have become angry, disappointed, and fed up, but it wasn't in his nature. The following year, the trees on the street all looked the same, each with an explosion of yellow flowers blossoming beneath them.

"Plant enough seeds, be patient. They will blossom," he would say. And he was right.

July 30th

🍎

Act: Be polite even when things aren't going your way, even when you may be annoyed.

Quote: "One cool judgment is worth a thousand hasty counsels." ~Woodrow Wilson

Reflection: A true testament of character is not reflected in the way we treat others when the sun is shining, the birds are chirping, and all of our grandiose plans are unfolding as expected, but rather in the seemingly chaotic moments that take us by surprise and throw us into a whirlwind of frustration, anger, and confusion. Slow down, stop, breathe, and remember— gentle words of love have a greater force than crescendos of rage.

Act: Have a neighbor you've been feuding with? Surprise them with a bouquet of flowers.

Quote: "Anything's possible if you've got enough nerve." ~J. K. Rowling

Reflection: I've found that it's the simple gestures that can inexplicably turn our biggest enemies into our greatest allies. We can argue over right or wrong, or take a step to make things right once again. We may live next door to someone, share the same driveway, share in conversation, but we never know the pain that exists in someone's heart, the true story of what goes on behind closed doors. There's no greater gift than the gift of understanding, the gift of empathy, and the gift of second chances, all of which don't need to be praised, don't need to be flaunted, just need to be given unconditionally.

August 1st

Act: Write inspiring notes on a few Post-Its and leave them at random places, from the bathroom mirror, lockers at the gym, or one of the pages of your favorite books at the library.

Quote: "In order to carry a positive action we must develop here a positive vision." ~The Dalai Lama

Reflection: When an endless string of questions plagues your mind, when you try desperately to find solutions to whatever problem you face, look for words of wisdom in the everyday things that surround you. Lyrics to a song, a sticker on a street lamp, chalk writing on the sidewalk, a billboard, or perhaps a sign in a store window. They are all calling out, reminding you of something you already knew to be true, but perhaps were frantically hoping to be told. So ask away and open your eyes wide enough to spot your answers in the seemingly mundane. They've been there all along!

August 2nd

Act: Pledge to do one thing today to make a complete stranger smile. Be creative. Hold a door open, tell a joke, or even laugh out loud.

Quote: "I guess sometimes the greatest memories are made in the most unlikely of places, further proof that spontaneity is more rewarding than a meticulously planned life." ~*The Edge of Always*, by J. A. Redmerski

Reflection: Within the first months of launching Life Vest Inside, I decided to organize a Kindness Mission Day. It would be a day about opening our eyes, hearts, and minds to connect a bit deeper with ourselves and those around us. As part of the mission, bags filled with a bunch of random objects were distributed to each team with instructions to figure out a way to use each object to make someone's day a bit brighter.

Although I would be overseeing the teams and not directly participating, I couldn't help but spot a public transit worker sitting alone grabbing a bite to eat. It looked as though she could use an extra bit of kindness that day. I searched within one of the mission day bags to find a thank-you card. I scribbled a note inside reading: "For service above and beyond the call of duty . . . Thanks!" and walked on over. She took the card and as she read it she started to cry, asking, "You got this for me?" Apparently it came at a time when she needed it most. She confided in me that she was feeling underappreciated, and was beginning to question whether her actions mattered. If we allow ourselves to become a listening ear, we open our lives to meaningful connections and inspiring moments.

Act: Compliment a coworker on something they excel at. Encouragement is the best way to show that you appreciate them.

Quote: "Delete the negative; accentuate the positive!" ~Donna Karan

Reflection: We all have our strengths and we all have our weaknesses. The way I see it, by simply acknowledging the strengths in another, we fill each other with the desire and yearning to transform our weaknesses into what can become our greatest assets. Constant negativity and focusing on someone's shortcomings make people doubt the things they were once certain of. Appreciation leads to gratitude, gratitude leads to confidence, and confidence leads to success.

I had a volunteer at Life Vest Inside who spoke English as a second language and it was clear that she was struggling with email correspondence, but her desire to succeed within the organization was apparent. I took a step back and began to pinpoint her greatest strengths. Once I found them and applauded her for her achievements, her attitude and excitement for the work she was doing grew tremendously. Above all she began to feel like a productive member of the team. Your ability to infuse confidence in the hearts of your staff is a great indicator of success.

August 4th

Act: Think of new creative ways to be kind today. Have an unlimited metro card? Swipe it for someone entering the station while you're on your way out. Let the creative juices begin to boil!

Quote: "I feel that there is nothing more truly artistic than to love people." ~Vincent van Gogh

Reflection: A good friend of mine, Lou, used to stop by his local 7-Eleven for coffee and a $2 scratch-off lottery ticket every morning. One morning he noticed an older woman paying for a few items with her welfare card. Lou looked down at the scratch off. He'd won $10.

He handed the ticket to the clerk waiting on the woman. "Take it from this. We're all here to help one another." She thanked him profusely and gave him a big hug. Overtaken by emotion, Lou sat in his car and began to cry; not because he chose to forgo his $10 scratch off, but because in that moment Lou caught a glimpse of the power of kindness.

August 5th

Act: Forgive yourself. We all make mistakes, we all fall short sometimes, but if you harp on errors of judgment you've made, you won't allow yourself to get up and take a step toward making things right. You are not your mistakes—you are better than that.

Quote: "To forgive is to set a prisoner free and discover that the prisoner was you." ~Lewis B. Smedes

Reflection: Too often we allow the fear of failure to paralyze us and prevent us from even taking the first step. The key is recognizing that success isn't determined by the absence of mistakes and hardships. Success is simply refusing to give in to the fear in spite of those hardships.

Here's to embracing fear and seizing the moment because you can!

August 6th

Act: Add yourself to a bone-marrow registry. Imagine if one day you find out that you're a match.

Quote: "Live today the way you want to be remembered tomorrow." ~Dillon Burroughs

Guest Reflection: We're all familiar with the phrase "You're a lifesaver"; a casual expression easily dispensed when picking up a friend from the train, offering to run an errand, or babysit. It's not every day that your phone rings and you're gifted with the opportunity to become a real lifesaver.

When I was approached at a local community fund-raiser to do a bone-marrow swab, I did what they asked and went about my day. A few months later I received a phone call from the registry informing me that I was a match for someone in need of a transplant. Further tests were made in the following months to confirm, but I finally got the phone call: "You're a perfect match!"

The day of the transplant I walked into the hospital as one person and walked out transformed. It was the greatest moment of my life, filled with the knowledge that I had saved a seventy-year-old woman suffering from Non-Hodgkin's lymphoma.

Every year the emotions rush back to me without fail as I receive my annual call from The Gift of Life Foundation letting me know that the woman is alive with no signs of recurrence. Five years down the road and she is still going strong. ~Ronette Chattah

August 7th

Act: Don't jump to conclusions. Give someone the benefit of the doubt. We all know what it feels like to be misunderstood.

Quote: "Nobody who is somebody looks down on anybody."
~Margaret Deland

Reflection: One day my mom rushed into the house screaming and ranting in disbelief. "I can't believe him! This is ridiculous. Of course, he can't pick up his phone. I had to walk all the way home in the crazy freezing snow."

Every morning my dad drove my mom to work and every day he would pick her up. But not that day.

We all took the offensive. "Dad, I can't believe you forgot to pick up Mommy. She had to walk the whole way home. She's freezing!"

My dad looked at all of us as my mom finished the last bit of her well-crafted speech she undoubtedly went over again and again in her mind during her long walk home. In the most calm demeanor he said, "But, Pauline—you drove."

Poor Mom—we'll never forget that one.

August 8th

♥

Act: What are you waiting for? Tell someone important in your life how much they mean to you. Life is short and you never know when it'll be too late.

Quote: "Friends are the most important ingredient in this recipe of life." ~Dior Yamasaki

Reflection: Stop making calculations as to the best time, best place, and best moment to share your feelings for another. Every moment is the right moment to tell someone you love them, you care for them, that they mean the world to you. Throw away the endless list of excuses. Whether it's "They already know how much I love them"; "Shouldn't they be the first to say it?"; or "Of course I love them! They know that!" And then there is the other form of excuses, the endless string of what if's. "What if they don't feel the same way?" "What if they don't care?" "What if I seem desperate?" "What if they ignore me?" "What if they hurt me?" What if? What if? What if? I say what if sharing your feelings opens the gates for them to reciprocate? What if they've been waiting to hear you say those words? What if this is your last chance to let them know how you feel?

Never be embarrassed for loving someone, be embarrassed for never letting them know.

August 9th

⬤

Act: Ask someone, "How are you?" Mean it and wait to hear their response.

Quote: "You never know the value of a moment until it is just a memory." ~Dr. Seuss

Reflection: Often we find ourselves asking the question, but rarely paying heed to the response. Let's fill our words with intent.

When my friend Debbie went out to walk her dog one random day, she didn't know a friendly hello would blossom into a meaningful friendship. Gladys could have nodded and walked on by, but she felt something especially touching and genuine about Debbie's greeting. Gladys was ninety-one years old, but sharp as a tack and craving something we are all in need of: some good old human interaction.

Perhaps it was Gladys's warm smile, her interesting perspective on a vast array of topics, the trivial chatter they would share about each other's family, or the fascinating stories she would tell infused with powerful life lessons, but Debbie felt an instant connection to Gladys from the moment she met her. Gladys enjoyed having a visitor but Debbie always felt that she was the lucky one. When Gladys passed, her wisdom remained in Debbie's heart and mind.

August 10th

Act: Traveling today? Take public transportation or perhaps set up a carpool. A great way to reduce traffic and an even greater way to help the environment.

Quote: "Sometimes it's not the journey or the destination, but the people you meet along the way." ~Nishan Panwar

Reflection: There are over seven billion people in the world. When asked about the importance of protecting the environment, many dismiss it feeling that it's not their problem, believing and trusting that someone else will find a solution, that someone else will fix it. Very often a lack of concern for the environment is due to the fact that people don't see the immediate impact it has on themselves and their family.

Impact isn't determined by the choices of others. It's an accumulation of our own choices, the small, barely detectable actions we take, the drops in the bucket we think will never matter all coming to a climax.

The simple act of taking public transportation can reduce our carbon footprint beyond our imagination when it all adds up.

August 11th

🍎

Act: Bake an extra batch of cookies to bring to work or send them with your child as a tasty treat for their teacher.

Quote: "Kindness is the golden chain by which society is bound together." ~Johann Wolfgang von Goethe

Reflection: She was the youngest of the volunteers at Life Vest Inside, but I've always known that age has nothing to do with capability. When Ida signed up to lead a group in our annual worldwide Dance for Kindness, I was certain that she would do a fantastic job. Empowering the group leaders who organize the event is my favorite thing to do; after all, without them the event simply doesn't happen.

From a distance it may look like I have everything under control, but everyone feels fear and hesitation. Perhaps I was the one that needed a bit of empowerment. Suddenly an unexpected package was left at the door. "You are doing amazing things! I know you must be tired, overwhelmed, and probably stressed, but keep going! This movement you started is truly inspirational. Here are some brownie-cookies that I made just to keep you going and to say WOW! This is incredible!"

Her faith in me helped me empower others. And the brownies were delicious.

August 12th

Act: Donate a week of your life to a cause dear to your heart. The possibilities are endless!

Quote: "We are here to add what we can to life, not to get what we can from it." ~William Osler

Reflection: In 2008, I headed to Israel as a chaperone on my first Chesed (Kindness) Mission Trip with the Yeshivah of Flatbush high school. For seven straight days, from early mornings until late evenings, I would be entrenched in kindness. From giving out gifts in orphanages, to playing dress up in hospitals, to preparing meals in soup kitchens, to singing and dancing my heart out with a group of special-needs children, to sharing stories with those living with blindness, to playing sports with a group of soldiers who lost limbs in battle; the experience was unlike any other. It was one of the most memorable trips I'd ever taken. I was inspired by these peoples' strength and determination, by the unwavering commitment to be happy in spite of hardships.

We may not all be fortunate enough to dedicate a week to a cause, but kindness doesn't come with a time limit or expiration date, it doesn't come with rules or restrictions. Give what you can, when you can, with all the heart you can.

Act: Take the time to return a lost object.

Quote: "Find a need and fill it." ~Ruth Stafford Peale

Reflection: Memory is a critical ingredient in the pursuit of a life of kindness. Recalling a moment when you too were in need, when you too were in search of the kindness of a friend, a stranger, or anyone who would take notice. Memory allows us to empathize, to connect, to step out of our comfort zone in the way we may have wished others would have. But memory holds with it a dangerous prospect as well. It can utilize the painful experiences and moments when we were forgotten, cast aside, or neglected to build an impenetrable wall around our hearts. The past can only retain its value and meaning if we put it to good use, recognizing that once the moments pass they are no longer easily categorized into buckets of right or wrong, but simply experiences that will assist us on our journey to become the people we were meant to be. So rise above. Not because you owe it to others, but because you owe it yourself.

August 14th

Act: Comfort a stranger who is crying. A few words of hope can be exactly what they need to restore their faith and assure them that everything will be okay.

Quote: "Behold the turtle. He makes progress only when he sticks his neck out." ~James B. Conant

Reflection: Life, like a roller coaster, comes with its ups and downs, thrilling moments that take your breath away and moments when you just wish it would stop, slow down, and let you take it all in. We're all accustomed to the extremes life throws our way, the great joy, inexplicable happiness, and the unfortunate grief, but it takes an extra special eye to see when someone else is on the downside of that spectrum of emotion. Life is about seeing yourself in someone else. It's about treating someone the way you want to be treated.

August 15th

Act: Do you know a colleague that is in a hospital? Take some time out of your day to visit, and while you're at it, grab a balloon to cheer them up!

Quote: "When you carry out acts of kindness you get a wonderful feeling inside. It is as though something inside your body responds and says, yes, this is how I ought to feel."
~Harold Kushner

Reflection: When I heard the news that Mrs. Orlow, a colleague, former teacher, and an all-time hero in my life had taken ill and was in the hospital, I knew it was time for me to act. Only a few months prior, we bumped into each other in the hall and shared common worries and concerns about making an impact on our students.

I wanted her to truly feel the influence she'd had, and so I collected letters of admiration from fellow colleagues, parents, former students, current students, and administration in a book and brought it to her in the hospital. I could tell that her heart was overflowing with gratitude. She thanked me profusely, and then she made me promise to read the letter I wrote at her eulogy when the day came for her to move on to the next phase of life.

Several years down the road, I opened my email to find a note saying Mrs. Orlow had passed. As I took the stand at her memorial service, I read aloud the letter I had written to her years before. I will forever be grateful that I didn't wait to share those words until that day and that she passed away knowing her true impact.

August 16th

❦

Act: Prevent someone from getting embarrassed. Discreetly let them know if they have something in their teeth.

Quote: "The friend who holds your hand and says the wrong thing is made of dearer stuff than the one who stays away." ~Barbara Kingsolver

Reflection: Do you ever wonder why people tend to overlook the great value in preventing something negative from transpiring? The real surge of excitement comes into play once mayhem has ensued. The "bat signal" flashing in the sky somehow calls to us and we feel more compelled to act and be celebrated as the hero of the hour. Here's something to consider. What is more heroic: running to someone's aid once the damage is done, or swooping in unnoticed to prevent that same person from ever feeling the stab of pain, hurt, or embarrassment? Let's begin to imagine how we would feel in someone else's shoes and the answer will suddenly become apparent.

August 17th

⭐

Act: Be true to yourself and remember you are the boss of your life! Wear your favorite color, speak from your heart, and live the life that feels best to you!

Quote: "If you can imagine it, you can create it. If you dream it, you can become it." ~William Arthur Ward

Reflection: The power to change your world is within your hands. Use your mind, trust your instincts, let your heart guide you, and watch how those intimidating mountains will magically flatten before your very eyes. Impossible is only a reality if you grant it the right to occupy your most valuable real estate—your thoughts.

August 18th

Act: Surprise a friend with a much-needed gift.

Quote: "I feel that the greatest reward for doing is the opportunity to do more." ~Dr. Jonas Salk

Reflection: While I would be dreaming out loud, Jeff, the mayor of Life Vest Inside's Kindness Ambassador group, would be taking notes to ensure that those dreams came true. I invested all my savings to build Life Vest Inside, but it never felt like a sacrifice; it felt like a privilege, an honor. But for many, it was baffling as to why someone would forgo a comfortable livelihood and be more inclined to give from their heart and their services without want of reward or compensation.

I've always been a hard-core Disney fan. Each story was another lesson to be learned, another dream to be dreamt. My cousins were planning a trip and I wanted to go, but money was tight. Without hesitation or question Jeff took action in his wonderfully sly way. When I opened the door that Tuesday morning I found an all-access Disney Park Hopper pass. Gratitude filled my heart.

August 19th

Act: Pick up the phone and make a daily check-in call to your mom or a close friend. Live together? Ask him or her how she's doing and see if there is something he or she might need today.

Quote: "Courtesies of a small and trivial character are the ones which strike deepest in the grateful and appreciating heart." ~Henry Clay

Reflection: Like clockwork, the phone rings at 9:05 am in the Wahba house. It's my grandma, my Nana!

Every morning without fail my mom and her two sisters are on the phone with Nana checking in. Nothing major has happened within the twenty-four-hour gap since they last spoke, but to Nana it means the world, and truth be told—it has come to mean that to her kids as well.

August 20th

♥

Act: Make a playlist of songs that remind you of a special someone and gift it to them. Include a small card letting them know how each song reminds you of them.

Quote: "You're like a song that I heard when I was a little kid but forgot I knew until I heard it again." ~Maggie Stiefvater

Reflection: Communicating wasn't my student Diane's strong suit. As a teacher it was my favorite pastime to see the beauty within my students so that they could eventually see it in themselves. It's why I became a teacher. But with each student the method of communication can be quite different. She wasn't able to express her thoughts and emotions verbally, and so music became Diane's voice.

Middle school was filled with hardship for her, but watching her grow into the person I knew she could be gave me the greatest pleasure. She gifted me with a CD expressing, through songs, how grateful she was to know that she could confide in me, knowing that as much as she may have tried to push me away I was there if she needed someone.

As the day of eighth-grade graduation approached, I prepared myself to let go knowing that it was time for her to move on to the next chapter of her life. All I could hope for was that the lessons she had learned in my classroom would stay in her heart and help her stay the course.

Whenever I pop that CD in, the memories fill my heart and I'm transported back to my classroom with the knowledge that I did leave an impression. Sometimes reassurance is all we need.

August 21st

☀

Act: Share the road! Be mindful of bicyclists and pedestrians.

Quote: "What this world needs is a new kind of army—the army of the kind." ~Cleveland Amory

Reflection: Life is all about perspective. How often do we find ourselves aggravated, frustrated, and annoyed during our morning commute? Motorists, bicyclists, and pedestrians all fighting to get to our destinations, pointing fingers at anyone and everyone we can blame for making the trip a bit longer than we'd like.

Let's begin to see the world through the perspective of the supposed person at fault and suddenly things won't seem as clear-cut as we first assumed.

We all have places to go, things to do, people to meet. With perspective comes understanding, compassion, empathy, kindness, and, finally, change.

August 22nd

Act: Do some research to learn about endangered species and make a contribution to ensure that they will be around for generations to come.

Quote: "There are two ways of spreading light: to be the candle or the mirror that reflects it." ~Edith Wharton

Reflection: Knowledge is only power if we are bold enough to apply it. And that power is most meaningful when it's in pursuit of building a better world and by protecting those who cannot protect themselves. Take a moment to think of ways we can impart kindness to those who do not ask.

August 23rd

🍎

Act: Make up with a friend today. We all make mistakes. Fighting isn't worth it.

Quote: "Forgiveness does not change the past, but it does enlarge the future." ~Paul Boese

Reflection: A second chance is difficult to dispense, but once given it has the unprecedented power to change you and teach you that there are always two sides to every coin. The more we can wholeheartedly accept people, mistakes and all, we find that our flaws are more readily forgiven. So today, instead of recalling the rare instances of strife and heartbreak, remember the moments of joy, laughter, and camaraderie shared.

August 24th

🌐

Act: Help a neighbor load or unload their car. Kindness, like a boomerang, always returns.

Quote: "Three things in human life are important. The first to be kind. The second is to be kind. The third is to be kind."
~Henry James

Guest Reflection: Like all great things, summer came to an end. After two amazing months staying with my in-laws, it was time to pack up and head back home. Moving can be stressful and exhausting, both physically and mentally. Our car was loaded and I was set to head back with my wife and son. Loading cars wasn't exactly the thing I loved doing most, but it was clear that my in-laws were far from finished. I rolled up my sleeves and got to work; it was the least I could do to show my appreciation and gratitude for what they'd given me. I didn't know it would turn into a pattern of giving from that day forward.

You can guess who was there ready to roll up their sleeves when it was time for my wife and our family to move into our new house two years down the road. A mover was out of the question for my father-in-law. Before I could even ask, there he was with my brothers-in-law ready and willing to lend a hand. The money I saved that day was far less valuable than the bonding and genuine connection that took shape. ~Joey Mansour

August 25th

Act: Offer to drive someone to the airport. What a great way to see them off on their travels.

Quote: "Little things seem nothing, but they give peace, like those meadow flowers which individually seem odorless but all together perfume the air." ~Georges Bernanos

Reflection: To many, airports are associated with stress and anxiety. But I've always found that if you look close enough you'll see the warmth that fills the hearts of those sending a loved one off or finally welcoming them home after a long and taxing journey. The smiles, the laughs, the tears, the hugs, the energy—it's magical.

Every year my family looked forward to our summer trip to Israel. The day after school ended, we hopped on a plane and the journey began. My brothers and I would anxiously push to get off the plane, our little bodies slipping through the crowds and our eyes scanning the sea of people. Finally we'd see him, Uncle Eli. As we ran into his arms we felt his energy and the warmth of his love.

Years later, after he passed away, I can still feel that magic every time I step off the plane in Israel. I hope he knew just how much it meant to us kids who were so deeply in love with him.

August 26th

Act: Vow to make a new friend today.

Quote: "The great difference between voyages rests not in ships but in the people you meet on them." ~Amelia Burr

Reflection: Appearing approachable and friendly is key to opening the door for exciting interactions to take shape.

So often we are afraid to approach others. Afraid to engage, to do the main thing humanity was built for—connect! Asking a simple question can change everything, though.

Vinay and I entered the train, smiled, and sat opposite one another. As I took my pad out to do some writing I had a funny feeling that Vinay and I wouldn't remain strangers for much longer. "What are you writing? A song? A poem?" he asked. Turns out I wasn't the only writer on the train—Vinay was a writer as well and we found out we had more in common than we thought. It was only a short fifteen-minute train ride but the exhilaration of forging a meaningful human connection is like no other. We were born to connect and no amount of technology will ever replace the need for physical face-to-face communication. Look up! Wonderful people are waiting to meet you.

August 27th

Act: Switch shifts with a coworker to help accommodate their schedule. You never know what may be going on in their life.

Quote: "The world is full of nice people. If you can't find one, be one." ~Nishan Panwar

Reflection: Kindness is found in the extra ounce of consideration we show to others when they need it most. Consideration has a funny way of returning to us at those very same moments of desperation in our own lives. It's precisely the instances when we have an excuse to justify our lack of consideration that our choices matter. Those decisions represent a true evaluation of who we are, what we believe, and how firmly we are willing to hold to those beliefs. If it were easy, kindness wouldn't be as rewarding as it is.

August 28th

✹

Act: Be kind to someone who has been unkind today. They often need it the most.

Quote: "A loving heart heals hate." ~Terri Guillemets

Guest Reflection: I had headed out to the mall to exchange a few items, and the cashier waiting on me seemed quite irritated and grumpy. She became frustrated as to why I didn't have exact change. I could tell that it was a rough day for her and I was simply in the line of fire. "I'm so sorry, I know it's a pain," I said calmly as I looked her in the eye. Suddenly I saw a change in her attitude and her face relaxed into a smile. She took a deep breath and explained that she was overstressed. I understood. We said our friendly goodbyes and I saw her demeanor shift as she continued interacting with others. It only takes a few genuine, heartfelt words to lighten someone's mood. ~Sonia Parekh, Dubai

August 29th

⭐

Act: Go for a stroll around your neighborhood.

Quote: "Looking at beauty in the world is the first step of purifying the mind." ~Amit Ray

Reflection: Leave your phone at home and take a deep breath of fresh air. Admire the world around you; nature, the city, the sky, the people, the feeling of letting go.

Taking the time to connect with nature and our surroundings, tech-free, can open us up and elevate us to levels of understanding far beyond any technology.

August 30th

Act: Think of something you usually let slide and exercise a bit more self-control for the day.

Quote: "About the only time losing is more fun than winning is when you're fighting temptation." ~Tom Wilson

Reflection: For some it's a diet. For some it's a substance. For some it's a person. But for all it's a struggle. Self-control is a coveted asset, and it takes time to develop. Don't give up on yourself so easily. One step at a time, my friend! Celebrate the small wins as you inch closer to your goal. The victory is not in the destination, but in the journey. You're doing great!

August 31st

Act: Call a family member and ask if they need some help running errands. Parking can be such a pain; plus, think of all the laughs you'll have.

Quote: "Never worry about numbers. Help one person at a time, and always start with the person nearest you." ~Mother Teresa

Reflection: Fridays are the craziest days in the Flatbush area of Brooklyn. With the Jewish Shabbat approaching and everyone out on the roads getting their last-minute groceries and errands done before sundown, finding a parking spot is almost impossible. Every week without fail, my sister Michelle heads out running errands and checking one thing off after the next for everyone and anyone in the family who asks, hoping to ease the burden of the pre-Shabbat rush. I wonder if she knows just how much I admire her for that. The small acts of kindness we do don't go unnoticed. They inspire others to follow suit or pass along the kindness in their own unique way.

September 1st

♥

Act: Plan an extra special surprise for a friend's birthday.

Quote: "Happiness is not something readymade. It comes from your own actions." ~The Dalai Lama

Reflection: A birthday is more than just a celebration of your day of birth, it's a reminder that you matter. I've never been a fan of my birthday, perhaps because it was a reminder that I was getting older, perhaps I was too afraid to get excited only to be let down if people didn't remember or it didn't turn out as special as I had hoped. But know this, even us closet "birthday haters" have a hidden hope that someone will make our day a special one. So take the extra time to celebrate someone special in your life because each person we meet is in fact a part of who we are.

September 2nd

Act: Make an effort to look people in the eye when you're talking to them. Give them your full attention.

Quote: "The soul's smile is found in the eyes' twinkle." ~Anna Pereira

Reflection: We live in a world of constant stimulation; everything and everyone is fighting to be seen and heard. Quality conversation, quality friendships, quality in general has been substituted for whatever provides the highest level of stimulus.

Ever take a step back to notice people in a crowded room? Often the way people interact with others is an indication of how they see themselves; a reflection of their insecurities, worries, and fears. For some people, living in the moment is something quite foreign. Fearful that they are missing out on something better, something more exciting, more relevant; they may be chatting with one person but their eyes are inconspicuously scouring the room to ensure that they aren't getting the short end of the stick.

Let's not measure a person by what they can give us or how much they can advance our careers. I say let's not measure at all, but simply enjoy being in the company of another, giving them the pleasure that for that time we see them and only them. Stop searching and start discovering.

September 3rd

❧

Act: Plan a day trip to a local park, garden, or forest. There's more nature close by than you may realize.

Quote: "Life is truly a reflection of what we allow ourselves to see and be." ~Trudy Symeonakis Vesotsky

Reflection: The solitude we can find in nature affords us the opportunity to strip away the worries that fill our minds, cloud our thoughts, and take hold of our hearts. Don't think of it as running away; think of it as finding your way back. You'll see that you'll discover more than just an appreciation for nature, but a deeper and more profound appreciation for life, imperfections and all.

September 4th

🍎

Act: Greet the maintenance staff in your school and thank them for a job well done. Find out their names (they are super awesome—you'll see!).

Quote: "We cannot live only for ourselves. A thousand fibers connect us with our fellow men." ~Herman Melville

Reflection: The first day of school in a new city is always nerve-wracking. Questions fill your mind. What will the other kids think of me? Will I ever find my place?

These questions and dozens more crowded my friend Jeff's mind as he made his way into a new school in Wyoming as a child. Luckily his mom was a teacher and knew her way around already.

"Jeff, say hello to Smiley; he's our janitor," his mother whispered to him. With one look, Jeff understood why Smiley was gifted with such a fortunate name. Receiving a warm greeting from Smiley each day was all the calm Jeff needed to tackle a new setting and find his place in it all.

It's no surprise that with the passing of Jeff's mom, Smiley found his way back into Jeff's life. They had a chance encounter at a sandwich shop, and Smiley regaled Jeff with story upon story about the inconspicuous kindness Jeff's mom had shown him.

When Jeff insisted that Smiley be a pallbearer at the funeral, Smiley gladly accepted. He was the first person to welcome Jeff's mom to her new school; how fitting that he too would be there to escort her to her final destination.

September 5th

Act: Leave a note of appreciation for your mailman.

Quote: "I've learned that people will forget what you said, people will forget what you did, but people will never forget how you made them feel." ~Maya Angelou

Reflection: We often check our mailboxes for letters, bills, and unexpected gifts without considering how they got there. A thoughtful note can leave your mailman with an extra bounce in his step as he makes his way through your neighborhood, rain or shine.

My mailman would always be bopping down the block, dancing to a song with a smile on his face, even if it was the coldest, dreariest day. He paid no heed to who was looking at him, but I was just one of the many commuters who caught a glimpse of his lighthearted cheerfulness and was mesmerized by the abundance of positivity radiating from his every step. Regardless of the mood I was in on a given day, I would smile, look up, take a deep breath, and know that as long as I had air in my lungs there was always reason to smile. It wasn't part of his job description as a mailman to be bright and cheery, but the things that separate us from others and make us stand out never are. The differences are always found in the small, seemingly insignificant things we do to brighten someone else's day.

September 6th

Act: Take notice of the expression on your face as you go about your day. A simple smile is all it takes.

Quote: "How slight a nod it would take, how bare a smile, to give everyone you meet today a sense of worth." ~Robert Brault

Reflection: We can all put on a smile, but for that smile to have the infinite impact that it's meant to have, to uphold its promise of being contagious in the most extraordinary way, it must go deeper and carry with it a piece of your very soul. Now take a moment and try to grasp the hundreds or thousands of impacts you can create daily—pretty wonderful, isn't it?

I think you'll find that it's precisely on the days when you question whether there is any reason to smile that smiling at another may just be the quick fix you need to put your questions to rest.

September 7th

Act: Write a touching, inspiring note and leave it on someone's windshield. A few kind words from a complete stranger can be the dose of kindness they were looking for.

Quote: "Happiness is a by-product of an effort to make someone else happy." ~Gretta Brooker Palmer

Reflection: A seed was planted when Karin's friend shared with her how an unexpected sticky note of goodness left on her windshield uplifted her and gave her hope after a rough day. As Karin drove home from work that evening and made a quick stop in a retail store, she couldn't help but notice the intense frustration around her. Shoppers let out sighs of aggravation and impatience, pedestrians shook their heads as cars raced by and ignored crosswalks, and drivers impatiently cut in and out of traffic, tailgating to get to their destination in the fastest possible way. She questioned, "Wasn't the holiday season a time of kindness and happiness?" She thought to herself, "Where there is sadness, worry, or irritation, there is always room for inspiration."

She set to the task of brightening windshields in parking lots throughout her area with sticky notes of positivity. Her notes lightened the spirits of those who were mysteriously targeted by the kindness vandal. And so her call for kindness vandals continues in hopes of inspiring each of us to blanket the world with kind words.

September 8th

✿

Act: Make a business introduction for a friend or fellow colleague.

Quote: "As we look ahead into the next century, leaders will be those who empower others." ~Bill Gates

Reflection: By helping others rise to achieve the dreams and goals they set for themselves, we advance our own ability to rise, becoming a leader who empowers others to find valuable skills and qualities within themselves. A true leader isn't threatened by another person's success. A true leader revels in the triumphs of others, understanding that victory is meant to be shared, not hoarded for one person's selfish consumption.

September 9th

Act: Take time to thank a strong, powerful woman in your life that has had a positive influence on you.

Quote: "As we express our gratitude, we must never forget that the highest appreciation is not to utter words, but to live by them." ~John F. Kennedy

Reflection: Growing up, reading was a continuous struggle for my friend Jeff, filled with frustration and anxiety. Words and numbers appeared inverted making reading assignments embarrassing and absolutely dreadful. That is, of course, until he met Mrs. Berry.

She never gave up on him. Instead she was patient and loving in her teaching method, providing Jeff with the confidence he needed and teaching him to slow down to better comprehend words. She helped him discover his passion for reading.

When his mother passed and Jeff began to think about those who've impacted his life in a positive way, Mrs. Berry was the first person that came to mind. Losing someone we love often forces us to pause and reflect on the lives we lead, the things that matter, and the people that make the journey worthwhile.

He called her up and shared the impact she had made on his life. That year was to be her last year teaching, but after her call with Jeff she changed her mind. "Your words have given me the strength to teach for one more year. Thank you for that." A few words of validation may provide someone with the motivation to keep pushing forward.

September 10th

✦

Act: Forgive and take a baby step to let go of the pain that someone has caused you. No, it's not easy—but it's necessary in order to make room for the good things that life has in store for you. Fill your heart with love, and there will be no more room to hate.

Quote: "The weak can never forgive. Forgiveness is the attribute of the strong." ~Mahatma Gandhi

Reflection: The pain and hardships we go through in life tend to connect us with a part of ourselves; an inner strength, an inner beauty that would otherwise remain dormant. But suppressed pain, prohibited from having a voice, can paralyze us and eat away at that very strength from the inside out. Being wronged hurts, but allowing that hurt to change who you are, to prevent you from going forward is far worse. The essence of forgiveness is, in fact, our ability to forgive—give forward in spite of the pain, recognizing that the more you give the more you truly heal.

September 11th

Act: Take the time to reflect. Begin your day with a private moment of silence.

Quote: "I've begun to realize that you can listen to silence and learn from it. It has a quality and a dimension all its own."
~Chaim Potok

Reflection: Sometimes silence is the most powerful sound of all. For me, today is a day of reflection. A day to reflect on where we want to be as a people, as global citizens of the world. The bit of light you share with the world through acts of kindness, generosity, compassion, love, tolerance, and acceptance are what inspire goodness to prevail. Let's take a moment of silence to reflect on those bits of good.

September 12th

🏠

Act: Kindly ask to borrow something that may be in your house but doesn't necessarily belong to you. Some say asking for forgiveness is better than asking for permission, but the way I see it, it's all about the way you ask.

Quote: "Receiving is good but giving is much better. Nevertheless, sharing is the best." ~Shahrizad Shafian

Reflection: I was never as much of a clotheshorse as my sisters. I had a date with someone and no matter what I tried in my closet, I couldn't find something appropriate. The perfect outfit finally came to mind; the only problem was it belonged to my sister. Lending out clothes is not something Michelle is known for. And, to top it all off, it was her favorite outfit.

The situation pretty much had "No way!" written all over it. But I figured I would try, and so I knocked on her door and explained, "I know how much you love this outfit and on top of that you have worn it only one time. But it would really mean so much to me if I could borrow it for my date tonight. If you say no, I completely understand." She paused. She could see it was important to me. She went to her closet, handed it over, smiled, and said, "Have a great time!"

Does asking always work? No. But I've found that when we're understanding even when the answer is "no," and when we are willing to lend things to others regardless of the countless no's we've received from them in the past, a shift is bound to happen. Change, the kind that matters, happens slowly and always with kindness.

September 13th

♥

Act: Pick up the phone, swallow your pride, and call the person you have been meaning to ask forgiveness from.

Quote: "Anyone can hide. Facing up to things, working through them, that's what makes you strong." ~Sarah Dessen

Reflection: You'll find that the more willing you are to dispense forgiveness, the greater ease you will have making the request yourself. Coming to grips with our weaknesses is never an easy task. It's no wonder so many of us tend to avoid those people who force us to stare at ourselves in the mirror. We are so fearful of what we may find behind the masks, layers, and walls we've so cleverly fashioned for ourselves. Afraid that we may end up simply staring at a person devoid of any real sense of strength, any real sense of accomplishment, and, worst of all, any real sense of worth. But you are not your mistakes. Your flaws can only define you if you give them the power to.

Then there are those of us who fear that our mistakes are too big to forgive, that our apologetic heart will be met with resistance and anger. All I can say is that there are no guarantees, but I, for one, have found that one kind word can erase even the most intense fury. Even if you're met with defeat, the likelihood is that you won't have any more trouble looking at yourself in the mirror.

September 14th

☀

Act: Take the time to return calls today, especially to those who may become upset or offended if you don't.

Quote: "True friendship is like sound health; the value of it is seldom known until it be lost." ~Charles Caleb Colton

Reflection: What makes us ignore a call or never return a call we've been meaning to make for so long? On the rare occasion it's simply bad timing, but for most it's apprehension about what that phone call may bring. An extra errand, time spent that we can't account for, an uncomfortable question that we don't want to answer. Ignoring an awkward phone call may seem to be the wise choice at the moment, but think of the repercussions, the countless awkward moments yet to come, and the unquestionable guilt that comes right along with it.

Procrastination never brings with it feelings of resolve. A person would rather you say that you're tied up, can't run the errand, don't feel like the relationship will work out, excuse yourself when you have to hang up, rather than act as though they don't exist. Is it easy? No, but it's worth it. We've all been on the receiving end of an unanswered, unacknowledged call; let's recall that emotion when the phone rings the next time on our end. You may not be able to answer, but a simple text can be all it takes to do the trick.

September 15th

Act: Take some time to learn a bit more about the human body and how it interacts and engages with the world.

Quote: "The two most important days in your life are the day you are born and the day you find out why." ~Mark Twain

Reflection: Take a moment to step outside and let the sun hit your face, or spread out in a park and read a book. When we engage our bodies with nature we are refueled, and this experience gives us a greater appreciation for the world around us.

September 16th

🍎

Act: Have you ever been the new kid at school? Then you might know the feeling of not fitting in or being lost. Next time a new student comes into your school, befriend them and show them the ropes.

Quote: "Friendship is born at that moment when one person says to another: 'What! You, too? I thought I was the only one.'" ~C. S. Lewis

Reflection: New settings bring with them the promise of new experiences, new opportunities, new friendships, and a renewed sense of our strengths. But the fear of the unknown can have the power to paralyze our ability to be who we truly are and let others in. A kind word, a friendly gesture, or a simple "Hey, my name is . . ." can melt away those fears and open the door for a new bond to ignite. Remember, fear is felt on both ends. So whether you're the newbie or the veteran, you'll need courage.

September 17th

Act: Put your skills to good use! Join a community mentoring program and mentor an at-risk child or teen. Perhaps all they need is someone to bet on them.

Quote: "Anything you're good at contributes to happiness." ~Bertrand Russell

Reflection: Joey, one of my students, was labeled by everyone as a bully and a troublemaker, and that's exactly what he became. He caused his fair share of trouble in my class, but I had seen the potential in his heart. It was only a matter of time until he would see it. As I was sitting in my classroom one day, I heard an argument in the hallway. I saw Joey standing there being reprimanded, yet again, by a teacher who had long ago written him off. There were talks of kicking him out of the school for good. I put my neck out and vouched for him, something no one had ever done before. I took him into the staircase to talk with him, hoping to finally break through the wall he built around his heart. Crying and in shock he yelled, "Why do you care so much? I'm so mean to you."

I smiled, looked him straight in the eye, and said, "Because I think the world of you and I only hope that one day you can see yourself through my eyes. So, you can push as much as you want to, but this is one person who will never budge." A spark was lit.

Now he's mentoring at-risk kids. When I approached him about it, he smiled and said, "You bet on me when no one else would. Everyone deserves to have someone bet on them."

September 18th

Act: Leave a few extra quarters at the Laundromat for the next person using the machine.

Quote: "It's the little details that are vital. Little things make big things happen." ~John Wooden

Reflection: The worst feeling is reaching into your pocket thinking you had four quarters to only come out with three. Use your change to make a change. After all, making a BIG difference begins with a small change.

September 19th

Act: Smile and show off that beautiful grin today. Pretty soon you'll notice people smiling back at you.

Quote: "Every time you smile at someone, it is an action of love, a gift to that person, a beautiful thing." ~Mother Teresa

Reflection: Heading out to work in the cold winter weather can be grueling, make us shut down, engage less, and become more easily agitated. To fight this, I like to play a game on my way to work. It doesn't take any extra time, cost any extra money, or get in the way of our everyday responsibilities. As I walk down the busy New York City block, I make it a point to connect with the eyes of each person I pass, as best I can, and smile. Most may not realize it; many may be caught up in their own world, but sometimes one person's day can be made better because of a smile from a stranger. Your smile may serve as a reminder to them of the things worth smiling for in their life.

September 20th

✿

Act: Clear up a dispute you're having with a coworker. Honesty is the best policy! Approach them with kindness and let them know how you're feeling. Communicate.

Quote: "Honesty without compassion and understanding is not honesty, but subtle hostility." ~Rose N. Franzblau

Reflection: For over two years, Life Vest Inside was simply me sitting in a small office working away on the computer. It wasn't sustainable, and worst of all it was pretty lonely. Then I was introduced to Charles by a mutual friend. He started off as an intern working one day a week, but I saw something in him and hired him on full-time.

The workload increased rapidly and I got so accustomed to calling Charles at any time because for me work never ended. He loved the cause and didn't seem to mind until the calls and workload became so overwhelming that Charles no longer had time for Charles.

One night as I was driving him to the train station, Charles decided to speak up. We never had a discussion like that in the past and it was new territory for the both of us. Confrontation is always scary. He began expressing how he was feeling: overworked, stressed, run-down. I began to become more mindful of the times I called him, how much I asked him to do, and the amount of gratitude I showed toward him. Sometimes the conversations we fear having the most are the ones we will look back on and ask what would have happened had we not. Communication is the glue that strengthens any and every relationship.

September 21st

Act: Find something positive to say about everyone and everything you encounter today. Looking for the good in others will bring out the very best in you.

Quote: "The way we experience the world around us is a direct reflection of the world within us." ~Ritu Ghatourey

Reflection: Perception is the way in which we cast our judgments, notions, and attitude on the world. Perceive beauty and you will see beauty. Perceive hatred, war, and aggression, and your perception will become your reality.

September 22nd

✦

Act: Go through an old notebook or journal. Look back and reflect. Share the memories with a loved one. Don't have a journal? Perhaps this will give you the push you've been looking for to start one. There's true healing power in writing down our thoughts.

Quote: "There's always room for improvement—it's the biggest room in the house." ~Louise Heath Leber

Reflection: Reflection is a key element to achieving and attaining success both in our personal and professional lives. If we continue to push forward each day without giving thought and credence to the past and where we've come from, what we've done, the mistakes and accomplishments we've made, it's easy to lose our way and fall off the path. Reflecting is merely a set of checks and balances for ourselves; it helps us stay the course and reminds us why we set out on the journey to begin with.

September 23rd

Act: Make a conscious effort to return money you borrowed from someone today. Whether you can pay it all back or only part of it, don't allow the fear of embarrassment of time gone by prevent you from doing what you know to be right.

Quote: "Respect for ourselves guides our morals; respect for others guides our manners." ~Laurence Sterne

Reflection: How often do we hold back from doing what we know to be right out of fear of being embarrassed? The longer we let time pass, the more we convince ourselves that the window of opportunity to right a wrong has come and gone and we have no choice but to live with an uncomfortable feeling in the pit of our stomach. Eventually we close our eyes to it completely, but, in our subconscious we hold tight to feelings of regret and remorse. Why subjugate ourselves to such emotions? Take courage, be brave, and do what you know in your heart to be right.

September 24th

🏠

Act: Focus on the positive! Practice giving heartfelt compliments to your siblings, spouse, parents, or friends.

Quote: "Be so happy that when others look at you, they become happy, too." ~Yogi Bhajan

Reflection: We are our own worst critics and more than likely are the first to be aware of our faults. One of the most difficult things is actually working on those traits, to only have those closest to us pick at them in the moments when we're not on our game. It can make us question whether anyone notices the positive strides we've taken and in the most unfortunate circumstances it can stop us from trying. Take a moment to cherish the positive things about someone close to you. Often if you encourage the positive, the negative falls away.

September 25th

♥

Act: Make up with a friend you're fighting with. Remember we all make mistakes.

Quote: "All I ever wanted was to reach out and touch another human being not just with my hands but with my heart." ~Tahereh Mafi

Reflection: A deeper reflection of our own deeds helps us see beyond the shortcomings and faults of another, recognizing those very same flaws within ourselves. We have all consciously or unconsciously caused pain to another. Do those feelings of pain negate all of the shared memories, the laughs, the tears, the support, the endless times the two of you were there for each other? Will we actually give free rein to our ego to do away with a friend simply because of a hurdle, or will we push through in spite of it with the knowledge that friendship is something worth fighting for.

September 26th

✹

Act: Been leaving someone hanging on an answer? Get back to them today.

Quote: "Procrastination makes easy things hard, hard things harder." ~Mason Cooley

Reflection: Closure is a coveted gift that people try to obtain, but many live their lives with the failed hope of attaining it.

Break the habit of procrastination. Put aside the worry that your answer is one they'd rather not hear. A response of any sort is better than no response at all. Your "no" may be the missing link needed for them to finally move on.

September 27th

❧

Act: Gift a plant to a friend or family member who has taken ill.

Quote: "A weed is no more than a flower in disguise." ~James Russell Lowell

Reflection: Life gives life. Love gives love. Kindness gives strength.

A plant carries with it healing powers; an energy that radiates light, warmth, and comfort. But the combination of the plant and the person who gifts it is where the magic lies, where the healing begins, and where strength takes root. It's a symbol that while some miracles are instant, the truly extraordinary go undetected. It begins by simply planting a seed.

🍎

Act: Human connection satisfies something completely different than Wi-Fi connection. We validate our friends and classmates on social media with likes, comments, and follows, but today validate a friend by picking up the phone and calling them.

Quote: "There is more to life than increasing its speed."
~Mahatma Gandhi

Reflection: In today's world of social media we are inundated with countless messages coming at us from a vast array of sources. Facebook, Instagram, WhatsApp, Twitter, Viber, Snapchat, text message, voice message. With all these forms of digital communication, it's no wonder there exists a lot of miscommunication. It seems as though we have lost the basic and most essential need of humanity—human connection. Perhaps our biggest fear is allowing people in, allowing them to truly see us, but speaking to someone can validate us in ways that nourish our soul far more than the validation we get from social media.

September 29th

Act: Help an elderly person across the street. Go ahead, ask their name and share a bit about yourself. A personal touch makes all the difference.

Quote: "Real unselfishness consists of sharing the interests of others." ~George Santayana

Guest Reflection: One day, as I was walking out of a store, I found myself caught in the middle of a downpour. I was living in Florida at the time where it frequently rains on summer afternoons. As I looked to my right, I saw an older woman without an umbrella. She searched around, and placed her purse on top of her head as she slowly started across the parking lot to her car. I thought to myself, "The only thing she is going to accomplish is getting her purse wet."

I opened my umbrella and approached her slowly so as not to startle her. I covered her with the umbrella and said, "Excuse me, ma'am, may I walk you to your car?" She smiled at me and clutched my arm as we made the slow journey to her car. During that time, I learned her name was Helen and she recently moved to the area from New York. She told me her husband recently passed, and she didn't have any family or friends nearby. When we reached her car, she grabbed my hand and thanked me. "This is the kindest thing anyone has done for me in a long time." A sense of purpose and connection washed over me as I walked away. I forgot completely about the dismal rain.
~Jeff Kuske

September 30th

Act: See someone eating alone? Ask to join them.

Quote: "Trust that little voice in your head that says, 'Wouldn't it be interesting if . . . ,' and then do it." ~Duane Michals

Reflection: The people we come across in our lives are there to teach us something. The question is, are our eyes opened to see it? It's pretty extraordinary how something as simple as a shared meal can bring with it feelings of joy, solidarity, and possibly a new friendship.

October 1st

Act: Join a Big Brother/Big Sister program in your community. You'll quickly learn just how much you have to offer simply by being you.

Quote: "All kids need is a little help, a little hope, and somebody who believes in them." ~Magic Johnson

Reflection: We can all use someone in our lives to make us feel special, make us feel important, feel as though we are their everything, and bet on us when we have no strength or confidence to bet on ourselves. For many, family is that someone. But then there are those who've had to fend for themselves and get through life without that built-in support system.

No matter the circumstances you come from, you can be that mentor for someone else so that they don't have to be alone. You can be the difference in one child's life and make them feel loved and supported.

October 2nd

Act: Set your alarm a little earlier and make a point to arrive on time today. Show others that you value their time by being punctual.

Quote: "The best way to get ahead is to get started." ~Mark Twain

Reflection: Time is one of the most valuable assets we possess. With only twenty-four hours in a day, seven days a week, and an unknown amount of days ahead of us, each moment, each second is yet another opportunity. The more mindful we are about squeezing the most out of every minute, the more opportunity lays before us to make use of that time for the common good. Appreciate the time of others and you'll receive the same in return.

October 3rd

Act: Start a jar of positive quotes or affirmations. Write down one positive affirmation or quote every day and add it to the jar. When it's full, think of someone that may need an extra pinch of positivity and gift it forward. Watch as the healing begins!

Quote: "You cannot have a positive life and a negative mind." ~Joyce Meyer

Reflection: Your thoughts and your mindset have the power to turn hopes and dreams into reality.

If you believe in the life you've imagined for yourself, you can achieve it. Shift the way you look at things and suddenly the things you look at shift. It's all part of the game of perception and you are the gamekeeper; you call the shots.

Your thoughts may not change the world, but they can change your world.

October 4th

✦

Act: Be kind to yourself today by counting your blessings. Make a Top 10 (or 25 or 100) list of things you're thankful for and share it with friends and family.

Quote: "Promise me you'll always remember: You're braver than you believe, stronger than you seem, and smarter than you think." ~A. A. Milne

Reflection: Uttering words of gratitude can change our whole outlook and has the power to draw great things into our life and give us even more reasons to be grateful. If you can't think of something to be thankful for, start with something very simple even if it seems silly. Once you start, finding other things comes easier.

October 5th

Act: Keep a daily log of good deeds. It will be a secret journal with yourself that you can look back on when you're feeling down.

Quote: "Find what makes your heart sing and create your own music." ~Mac Anderson

Reflection: My journal gave me more than just a few moments of solace at the end of my day; it gave me an opportunity to reconnect with myself, my goals, the person I am, and the person I want to become. Recording my actions allowed me to see my intentions and motivations, teaching me about myself and providing me with tools that allowed me to take strides in the right direction going forward.

Examine with introspection and you will have the courage to acknowledge whether your actions come from the right place. Set aside this invaluable time and head out on a personal exploration equipping yourself with the tools needed to rise to who you want to be. Don't fret about what you find. It's simply the first step in the process.

October 6th

🏠

Act: Offer to do the dishes. It may not be your turn or even something common in your household, but a simple gesture and action on your part can say "I love you" without a word.

Quote: "People may not always tell you how they feel about you, but their actions will speak for themselves." ~Ash Sweeney

Reflection: Ever wonder why the word "chores" is used for household tasks like doing the dishes? The word alone can do the trick of making someone see the task at hand as an insurmountable obstacle that will drain all of your energy. Imagine if we saw chores as moments to show gratitude, love, and to nurture appreciation. Suddenly, tidying up or helping someone take out the trash feels like something we're doing because we care about that person. It can even be a chance to spend meaningful time with someone while you're helping him or her. Make it a group activity, turn on your favorite music, and have some fun.

October 7th

♥

Act: Know someone going through a rough patch? Fill a box with some of their favorite treats and ship them a care package.

Quote: "The paradox of gifts: I know what I have given you. I do not know what you have received." ~Dr. SunWolf

Reflection: Regardless of how many times I've done it, I always get nervous before speaking publicly. Before heading out to give a talk, my friend Jeff called to give me a pep talk. "If you find yourself getting nervous, just picture me sitting front and center wearing my favorite Hawaiian shirt, and remember the crowd is rooting for you to succeed." From that moment all I needed to do was picture my dear friend Jeff in his favorite Hawaiian shirt and suddenly I knew it would all be okay.

The morning of my thirty-third birthday marked the first day I was able to get out of bed in several weeks after intensive oral surgery. Being stuck in bed is particularly hard for me as thoughts and feelings of being useless and unproductive run through my mind. I was down on myself that morning until the doorbell rang and I opened it to find a package. Jeff, in his own sneaky way, had sent a birthday gift to me. I ripped open the package to find Jeff's Hawaiian shirt folded neatly. In that moment I knew it would all be okay.

October 8th

✺

Act: In conversations today, be mindful of saying the person's name when greeting them and don't forget to make eye contact.

Quote: "A person's a person, no matter how small." ~Dr. Seuss

Reflection: Knowing someone's name can be the difference in that person feeling seen or not. Whether it's a coworker, a classmate, someone in your community, or the support staff at your office or school, these people deserve your attention and kindness. A simple hello, smile, or brief introduction can make someone's day and maybe even lead to a friendship.

October 9th

❧

Act: Plan a fun outing to a local orchard with family or friends.

Quote: "What you plant now, you will harvest later." ~Og Mandino

Reflection: When I was a kid, all week my siblings and I would anxiously wait for the weekend. It wasn't the notion of a day without school that excited us. We were up at the break of dawn, dressed, ready to go, and sitting patiently by the window waiting for the honk of his horn. My uncle Jack: the biggest kid of all. He'd have a huge smile on his face and bags full of treats in the backseat of his car. My siblings and I hopped in to join our favorite people in the world: our cousins, our family. Looking back, I don't think it would've mattered whether we went for a drive around the block or a cross-country road trip, we were exactly where we wanted to be. For Uncle Jack it was all about togetherness. We all felt his love, he made sure of that. Every Sunday another outing, another adventure, another excursion, and, most important, another day to connect, smile, and take in all that life had to offer.

Apple picking was one of our all-time favorites. The warm aroma of apples, the brisk feeling in the air, and the great wonder that filled this little fruit.

An apple was no longer a fruit, it was a tool that instantly transported me back to that day, that time, that car ride, and the love we all felt from just being together, just being us.

October 10th

🍎

Act: Bring a healthy treat or a batch of cookies to the security guard in your school.

Quote: "The manner of giving is worth more than the gift." ~Pierre Corneille

Reflection: When my fourth-grade teacher assigned us a project to write about an everyday hero, one person quickly popped to mind. We called him Tony the Tiger, and he was the school security guard. Tony was one of the kindest people I knew. Every morning as I walked into school, he would greet me with his warm smile. As a kid, I had a lot of anxiety about going to school, and stepping out of my mom's car in the morning wasn't as simple a task as you would think. But Tony had a special way about him; he was able to melt away my fear and make me feel safe. I'll always remember the joy on his face when I gifted him a box of home-baked cookies and a copy of my assignment.

October 11th

Act: Reach out and welcome someone new to your community, class, or apartment building.

Quote: "A 'me society' is selfishness. A 'we society' is kindness."
~B. D. Schiers

Reflection: The sign of a great community is one in which people feel empowered to be who they are. The same is true of a great leader. In 2013, I launched the Kindness Ambassador program. On top of members receiving weekly kindness tasks, they had the opportunity to connect with one another on a closed Facebook group. The amount of love, respect, and kindness amongst members of the group is touching and with each day it continues to grow with new members joining from all around the world. Rosie, one of the Ambassadors, didn't have the official title of Welcome Counselor, but her actions and the way in which she made members of our online community of Kindness Ambassadors feel awarded her that title. Rosie's natural ability to embrace people transformed the dynamic of the group and went as far as inspiring even our most reserved members to shed their insecurities, share their voice, and let others in.

October 12th

Act: Look up at the sky. Regardless of whether you believe in God, or something else for that matter, it's important to pause, take in the bigger picture, and be grateful for the life that is within you.

Quote: "Nothing can dim the light that shines from within."
~Maya Angelou

Reflection: We each face our battles, but reveling in our wins and expressing gratitude for the moments of happiness that have come our way will make these battles easier to conquer. The vision and yearning to see the beauty has the potential to clear the darkness from our eyes so that we may see a bigger picture and realize these moments of happiness are part of something grander.

October 13th

Act: Place a $10 bill inside the DVD case you are returning to Redbox or Netflix with a note saying, "Movie snacks are on me."

Quote: "No person was ever honored for what he received. Honor has been the reward for what he gave." ~Calvin Coolidge

Reflection: When we envision ourselves on the receiving end of an unexpected act of kindness, we can begin to catch a glimpse of the happiness and exhilaration it brings. But even more meaningful is the inspirational story that will be recounted for years to come and enact future acts of kindness. A small gesture can turn a great movie into an even greater story.

Act: Work can be frustrating and we all have tough days. Take a moment to breathe. A small breath can bring things right back into perspective.

Quote: "Happiness comes from . . . some curious adjustment to life." ~Hugh Walpole

Reflection: Every person is a conduit to bring something special into the world. The more we care for our conduit, the more goodness can flow through it to reach its destination.

I had just gotten back from a twelve-hour flight, feeling exhausted and dirty. All I wanted to do was take a nice, warm shower. When I got home I turned my shower on and was disappointed to see that the water was just dripping out of the showerhead. I told my dad that we had a water pressure issue, but after a bit of careful examination, turns out it had nothing to do with the pressure. My dad explained that the showerhead just needed a good cleaning. "A cleaning?" I thought. "You can up the pressure as much as you want, but that won't make more water come out of the nozzle without a cleaning," he said. With the continuous flow of water over time, mineral deposits build up in the shower head causing the nozzle to clog up.

Life is hectic. With all the running around and continuous strain we place on ourselves, we need a moment to take a breath and refresh, allowing us to clear out all the wear and tear that builds up with daily stresses. We may want to turn the pressure up in hopes that it will help us produce, but often the greatest cure is nothing more than a breather.

October 15th

❦

Act: Write a letter to the manager of a store you frequently visit extolling an employee's good service.

Quote: "Unexpected kindness is the most powerful, least costly, and most underrated agent of human change." ~Bob Kerrey

Reflection: Acknowledgment can have a profound impact. Retail and food service jobs can be thankless, with crazy schedules, long hours, and the endless frustrations and criticism from unhappy customers.

A few words of gratitude can instill a sense of pride not only for the employee, but the entire business, and start a wave of kindness.

October 16th

★

Act: Write a love letter to yourself.

Quote: "Self-love has very little to do with how you feel about your outer self. It's about accepting all of yourself." ~Tyra Banks

Reflection: Often we find ourselves seeking validation from external things like wealth, popularity, physical beauty, etc. But those external things will never fill the void within us all that craves genuine validation. True validation comes from loving yourself. Recognize that you matter, that you are significant, and that even though you might be one in seven billion people, the number that matters the most is that you're one. Only once you begin to see it within yourself will others see it as well. You are worth it.

Act: Send a condolence card to someone who has recently lost someone.

Quote: "Wherever a man turns he can find someone who needs him." ~Albert Schweitzer

Reflection: Loss is inevitable, but it still creeps up on us. No one can ever fully prepare for losing a loved one. When the time comes, some of us are left shattered, some of us are left in shock, and some of us are simply lost somewhere in between. Unaware of what to feel, what to say, what to think, or how to move on. With emotions running high, the outsider may question their right to be present, their right to show affection, their right to offer comfort. In fact, there are no magic words to be said, no rhyme or reason to be made, no justification to be found. All there is, is you. Be present, so that when that person emerges from the whirlwind of despair they will have someone to lean on.

October 18th

🏠

Act: Help your sibling, cousin, niece, or nephew with their homework and really commit to it with a smile. Performing an act of kindness as though we are sacrificing our time takes the beauty away from the power of the act.

Quote: "Helping others isn't a chore; it is one of the greatest gifts there is." ~Liya Kebede

Reflection: The peer-tutoring program in my community matched up people with kids that needed tutoring but couldn't afford the expense. A bunch of my friends and I were involved in this program, and one night when we were all hanging out, my friend Mark's younger brother walked in and asked for help on his math homework.

Mark said that now wasn't a good time because he was busy hanging out with friends, and his younger brother started walking away, disappointed and frustrated. Just then Mark's phone rang. It was the peer-tutoring program calling to let him know that they needed him to fill in for someone. "Of course, I'll be there right away . . . Not a bother at all!" Within a few minutes, he headed out the door, his brother overhearing the entire conversation.

Doing good for others is wonderful, but if kindness simply remains an action as opposed to a mindset, its true power to transform us into more sensitive and aware individuals goes unfulfilled. Keep your eyes peeled. You don't need to go far to see opportunities for kindness. Many times they are right within your own home.

October 19th

♥

Act: Schedule a board-game night with your cousins, siblings, or friends and enjoy some good old clean fun. You are a huge part of their foundation just as they are a huge part of yours. Make it a night to remember.

Quote: "Life is a song—sing it. Life is a game—play it." ~Sai Baba

Reflection: It was Sunday night and I had loads of work to get done. I had become known as a workaholic. Don't get me wrong, the work I do is something I love; connecting with people, making an impact. It's addictive in its own way, but at times it can also be overwhelming. The only way to get it all done was to schedule myself by the minute. According to my schedule I should be sitting upstairs in my home office typing away. I had a choice to make, stay upstairs and continue to work, or head downstairs and enjoy some family time. The sounds of laughter drew me downstairs and I spent the next couple of hours playing a game of Settlers of Catan while enjoying the company of my family.

Taking the time to reminisce often grants us a much clearer and more accurate perspective of where we're heading in life. I've long ago forgotten what tasks remained on my list that day.

October 20th

✸

Act: Next time you see a street performer, stop, take a moment to enjoy the performance, and give them some change in support.

Quote: "Art is not what you see, but what you make others see." ~Edgar Degas

Reflection: As I stood back to see the reactions of those intently watching, the smiles, the laughs, the excitement, the wonderment—I realized this street performer was providing these onlookers with respite from the challenges, worries, and anxieties of their day. He may not have changed their lives, but in that moment he changed their attitudes, and that is everything.

October 21st

✦

Act: Pledge to recycle your e-waste. Every year, thousands of old electronic devices are thrown into landfills, polluting the environment. Take the pledge and become part of the change.

Quote: "Being good is commendable, but only when it is combined with doing good is it useful." ~Stephen King

Reflection: While one person considers something garbage, another person considers its hidden potential. The difference is that of perspective; perception of the possibilities that are yet to be discovered. Remove the blinders and open your eyes. You may be pleasantly surprised by what you find.

October 22nd

🍎

Act: Bring an extra snack to school today and share it with someone who may not be in your group of friends.

Quote: "Remember that the happiest people are not those getting more, but those giving more." ~H. Jackson Brown, Jr.

Reflection: I've found that by simply preparing ourselves to embrace a wonderful opportunity, such an opportunity will magically present itself.

Who knows? Years from now, when asked how you met your best friend, you just may say that it all began with a Fruit Roll-Up.

October 23rd

Act: Eat and shop locally today. Local storeowners could use your support to keep their businesses alive and thriving. Help them on their journey to success.

Quote: "Every single time you help somebody stand up you are helping humanity rise." ~Steve Maraboli

Reflection: Mosaics is a small restaurant with a big heart. You instantly feel welcome when you walk through the doors. The concept is simple, but brilliant. There are no prices on the menu. That's right, no prices. All that's required is a $10 donation for each meal and a smile to go with it. Have more to give? Great! In Mosaics you can donate a meal to someone else. Have less? No explanations required. Have nothing? Take on a unique opportunity to earn your meal by offering an hour of service.

At Mosaics it's not about how much you give, it's simply about giving something; acknowledging that everyone has something to give regardless of how much is in their wallet. Hope and dignity—those are the two magic ingredients Mosaics gifts to every customer.

October 24th

Act: Let a fellow driver merge into your lane.

Quote: "It is the greatest of all mistakes to do nothing because you can only do little—do what you can." ~Sydney Smith

Reflection: Driving can be stressful and hectic, especially when in a rush. See someone signaling to merge into your lane? Don't turn your head pretending you don't see them (let's be honest, we all do that). Let them cut in front of you. And, hey, you might as well wave while you're at it.

The common courtesy we give to others will find its way back to us in times when we need it most. A simple ten-second investment has the potential to ease the stress of others and in its own mysterious way bring a great deal of peace back to you.

October 25th

Act: Next time you hop into a taxi, start up a friendly conversation with the driver; they have the most interesting stories to tell.

Quote: "Kind hearts are the gardens, / Kind thoughts are the roots, / Kind words are the blossoms, / Kind deeds are the fruits." ~Henry Wadsworth Longfellow

Reflection: For many a taxi is simply a means of transportation, taking you from one place to the next, but a few kind words can give your trip more meaning and, on occasion, give you a great friend.

When George picked me up at 1:00 pm to head to the city, his only caveat was that he had to be back in Brooklyn by 4:30 pm for an important appointment. I knew I was dealing with a tight timeframe, but I've always been one to live my life by the minute. "We'll make it!"

I hadn't planned for the guests of the wedding I was catering to be late or for an excruciating tooth pain to accompany an already stressful day. I could barely speak, let alone stand on my own two feet. Seeing how sick I'd become, George rushed me to the doctor while trying his utmost to make sure I was as comfortable as possible. Four thirty had come and gone, but George didn't leave my side for a moment. We tend to categorize people by the job titles they have. George isn't just a driver, he's one of the most kindhearted, caring people I've had the pleasure of meeting. Who we are is far more important than what we do.

October 26th

❊❊

Act: Mentor a new coworker and show them the ropes.

Quote: "When I was young, I admired clever people. Now that I am old, I admire kind people." ~Abraham Joshua Heschel

Reflection: Our experiences are meant to teach us, but they are also gifts given to us so that we can teach others and guide them along the path to self-discovery. A true leader and teacher isn't saddened when his or her time to lead comes to an end. A true leader basks in the glory of his apprentice and takes pride in his handiwork; cheerful when the day comes for the apprentice to take the reins.

Each person has something unique they can pass on to another. Don't allow the painful struggles you've endured alone and unguided to harden your heart and turn an eye from someone who can now benefit from the rough road that you tread and the smooth path that you paved in its place. You have manned your ship amazingly. Now it's your turn to share your maps, so that those you're guiding can steer the ship with confidence and dignity.

You may not always receive the credit, but then again a true leader isn't in it for the credit; the impact is what matters most.

October 27th

Act: Offer to visit or assist someone who is struggling with a life issue.

Quote: "How far that little candle throws his beams! So shines a good deed in a weary world." ~William Shakespeare

Reflection: While on disability from a heart procedure, Lee's unexpected encounter with a man dying from ALS changed the whole course of her recovery.

He had four children and a wife who cared for him, and for a few weeks, visiting the family became part of Lee's routine. A few weeks later, she found herself living with them and caring for the father as he approached the final stages of the disease. Giving away everything she owned in her two-bedroom apartment, she moved into their basement, and learned the process of caring for someone with ALS to help the wife and family. She refused any compensation. Below is a note she wrote on her experience.

"I had developed a deep relationship with the wife, kids, and especially the father. It was hard to see a father sitting in a chair without the ability to hug and kiss his wife and children. Because of his strong faith in God, he never complained. He taught me so much about life through his slow death, without saying a single word. The family and I were all together when he took his last breaths, later that summer. As sad as it was to see him go, the joy penetrated our hearts because he was no longer suffering such a terrible disease. His testimony through dying ignited a fire within me to love unconditionally. I consider that the ultimate gift of kindness."

October 28th

★

Act: Who says you can only do spring cleaning in the spring? Take some time to reorganize your space.

Quote: "One of the advantages of being disorderly is that one is constantly making exciting discoveries." ~A. A. Milne

Reflection: Clearing up physical clutter clears out our mental and emotional clutter as well and lets us start fresh. Who knows, you might find something to donate that will enrich the life of another.

October 29th

Act: Give someone a second chance. It's something that takes a lot of effort. But you will have ended up gaining far more than what you've given.

Quote: "It often takes more courage to change one's opinion than to stick to it." ~Georg Christoph Lichtenberg

Reflection: A real second chance is one free of judgments and expectations from the past; one that allows a person to be reborn as if from new. By holding tight to the pain someone caused you and casting feelings of doubt, expecting them to disappoint you, you are simply paving the way for that disappointment. Tip: Think of the good experiences you've shared. We tend to focus on the negative moments; the fights, the mistrust, the heartache, that we pay no heed to all the laughs, joy, and memories created with that very same individual.

October 30th

🏠

Act: Say "please" and "thank you" today in your home and really mean it! There is a reason they are called the magic words!

Quote: "Appreciation is a wonderful thing. It makes what is excellent in others belong to us as well." ~Voltaire

Reflection: Acknowledgment is the true essence behind these two phrases. Acknowledge that someone cares about you, is there for you, and, most important, "sees" you. How often we utter these words without giving credence to just how powerful they truly are. Take the time to look into a person's eyes as you say these wonderful words of appreciation and gratitude. Remember, without giving our words true meaning, they are simply syllables brought together to create a sound.

October 31st

♥

Act: Search for the good in someone who you may have misjudged.

Quote: "Rock bottom became the foundation on which I rebuilt my life." ~J. K. Rowling

Reflection: Goodness is inherent in each and every individual. The quest to uncover goodness is where the challenge lies. For some, goodness can be spotted from the very moment you meet them, for others goodness is hidden away, but it exists deep in the recesses of their soul waiting, hoping, yearning for someone to help them see it again in themselves. Mistakes are part of life. Choices we shouldn't have made, things we shouldn't have said, and actions we shouldn't have taken. But remember this well, our mistakes do not define who we are, it's how we respond to them that does. If we allow them to take hold of us, we may no longer believe that we merit redemption, that we merit a second chance; we rob ourselves of the possibility of what could be.

Let us search a bit further, dig a bit deeper, embrace a bit stronger the idea that change can only begin when we allow ourselves to see that a person has the potential to change.

November 1st

*

Act: Make an effort to look people in the eye when you're talking to them and give them your full attention.

Quote: "Eye contact is way more intimate than words will ever be." ~Faraaz Kazi

Reflection: More important than the time we spend conversing with another is the quality of the connection we infuse into those moments. Are we simply physically there, or do we see beyond the outside noise, the countless distractions, to see each person as a world of their own.

November 2nd

Act: Spend a little extra time with your pet. They miss you dearly when you're out and about at work or running errands.

Quote: "Sometimes the answer to our prayers is to become the answer to someone else's prayers." ~Robert Brault

Reflection: As Jeff and his friends stood on the porch one rainy evening, he heard something. There lying under a car sat The Captain, a small six-week-old kitten lost and afraid. As Jeff lifted him up, the kitten curled up in his arms and began to purr. Jeff decided to take him in. During the first week they spent together, Jeff did what he could to help The Captain readjust, trying to reassure him that he was safe and protected. But the feeling of abandonment is not an easy feeling to shake. The following week Jeff headed back to work but when he returned home he learned that The Captain wasn't quite as adjusted as he had hoped. Running, scratching, biting, and acting up were the only things The Captain knew. The Captain looked at Jeff with his wide eyes as if to say, "Where did you go? Why did you leave me?"

Jeff knew how it felt to be abandoned and lonely and so he worked even harder to ease The Captain's worries. The time he spent with this little kitten each day, comforting him, became the time of day Jeff looked forward to the most.

November 3rd

🍎

Act: Have a major test coming up? Surprise your classmates by preparing a review sheet for them.

Quote: "Getting the most out of life isn't about how much you keep for yourself, but how much you pour into others." ~David Stoddard

Reflection: The time and effort we invest into strengthening others is never wasted, but rather it propels us to even greater heights than we may have initially expected. Our successes are not simply measured by what we physically achieve but by the collective whole of what we can help others achieve. It is only once we let go of the false notion that one must fall for another to rise that we can fully appreciate that the achievements of someone we supported are, in fact, our very own.

November 4th

Act: Copy your favorite recipe and share it with a friend or neighbor. We put so much love into our food, why not share it? Perhaps include a sampling with it.

Quote: "Life isn't about getting and having, it's about giving and being." ~Kevin Kruse

Guest Reflection: Grilled chicken chili was my coworker Glenda's all-time favorite food. Without fail, she would insist on a second bowl to take home for dinner.

Cooking is a love of mine and love is always meant to be shared, so one day I left a heaping bowl of chili on her desk for when she came into work. Taped to the bottom of the bowl was a copy of the recipe. Nothing thrilled me more than the expression on her face, the delight and the gratitude. I can still feel the warmth of her embrace as she ran over and gave me a hug.

Fast-forward a couple of weeks down the road. I received an unexpected call and a heartfelt thank-you. She lit up as she shared the experience of cooking a tasty bowl of chili for her boyfriend. The gift of food is one of the most intimate gifts we can give. Food not only nourishes the body, it nourishes the soul. ~Jeff Kuske

November 5th

Act: Borrowed someone's car? Fill it up with gas. Whether it's your parents,' your friend's, your boss's, and yes, even your younger sibling's.

Quote: "Always be a little kinder than necessary." ~James M. Barrie

Reflection: I was running super late to an important meeting. I grabbed the keys, my laptop, and the presentation I had been working on endlessly. I was always nervous about speaking publicly—what if I lost my stream of thought, what if my words didn't leave an impact on the audience, what if I failed? There was no time to spare. As I jetted into the car, I saw it lying on my steering wheel. A Post-It note with a few words scribbled on it. "Thought I'd fill it up for you. Knock 'em dead. And remember, I believe in you." That one small note and gesture changed my whole outlook.

November 6th

Act: Take a jacket you never wear and give it to someone on the street (go ahead and do this with anything you haven't worn in the past six months).

Quote: "People seldom notice old clothes if you wear a big smile." ~Lee Mildon

Reflection: A simple action, a simple idea put into play can grow further than we ever expect. I've found that one good deed almost instantaneously leads to another. Merely being engaged in an act of kindness, an act of giving, awakens an awareness within ourselves to begin seeing more and more opportunities with every step we take. But the greatest impact our acts of kindness make is on the lives of those who observe from a distance; watching the excitement, motivation, and drive that we radiate in the midst of our giving spree. It may not always be evident, but your positive actions inspire others to follow suit. It may start with sifting through your old clothes and gifting them to others.

November 7th

✿

Act: Do you know a coworker who is out sick? Send them a get-well card. All that positive energy just may be the medicine they need to make a full recovery.

Quote: "Happiness can be found, even in the darkest of times, if one only remembers to turn on the light." ~Albus Dumbledore

Reflection: Recognizing when someone is absent reassures them that their presence matters. We all want to matter, to believe that we bring something unique into the world, that by us simply showing up we impact change and touch people.

The world may have us believing that we are dispensable, and although time goes on with or without us, our actions, our interactions, and our choices leave an impression. It may be subtle, but it's there. We all may not be as fortunate as George Bailey from *It's a Wonderful Life,* privy to a glimpse of a world without us, but be confident that although the day will go on— the difference is in the details.

November 8th

🦋

Act: Spend some time sharing your knowledge and skill set with someone who needs it.

Quote: "The greatest good you can do for another is not just to share your riches but to reveal to him his own." ~Benjamin Disraeli

Reflection: Be it driving, playing an instrument, using a certain computer program, photography, cooking, or anything in between, talents are meant to be shared.

Technology and computers were never my thing. Once I met Travis all that changed. He had a great way of breaking things down and introducing me little by little to new platforms, technologies, and apps that made starting a business so much more seamless. But what Travis doesn't know is that he didn't simply teach and empower me, he taught all of the hundreds of people that I now have the pleasure and fortune of handing that knowledge over to. With every email, every Facebook message, every phone call I receive thanking me for taking the time to help someone learn something new that made their life just a bit easier, I think of Travis and I smile.

November 9th

✦

Act: Smile at yourself in the mirror for fifteen seconds. Tell yourself you are beautiful (you are!).

Quote: "No one can make you feel inferior without your consent." ~Eleanor Roosevelt

Reflection: Regardless of what physical traits you see staring back at you, look deep into your eyes, and what you will find is the most special and beautiful prize of all—your unique and wonderful soul. You are beautiful.

November 10th

Act: Think of one positive action or activity you can do on a regular basis and begin doing it today.

Quote: "It is not because things are difficult that we do not dare; it is because we do not dare that they are difficult."
~Lucius Annaeus Seneca

Reflection: When I tripped on that September morning as I ran into school to take cover from the rain, little did I know my hopes of playing basketball in senior year were over. I had been on the basketball team ever since middle school and I loved it. Sports were a big part of who I was but they also dominated my after-school schedule.

As I crutched out of the doctor's office, I wondered what I would do now. My friend was constantly inviting me to volunteer at Sephardic Bikur Holim, a local organization focused on providing aid for members of the community. I finally joined and started attending weekly meetings. The passion and excitement that filled me every time I saw a smile on the face of a person I went to visit in a hospital or old-age home and the joy that filled the hearts of the children when they received a bag of toys on the holiday made me fall in love with the mission of kindness.

November 11th

🏠

Act: Take the time to really listen today. Someone in your own home may need to talk.

Quote: "Having a place to go is home. Having someone to love is family. Having both is a blessing." ~Donna Hedges

Reflection: How many times have we outwardly said, "I'm fine! It's all good!" while inside we were truly a mess? I have always been a pro at that. It's not often that people see beyond the words and understand the feelings.

It was the Passover holiday and my family arrived at the house for what is usually one of my favorite gatherings. I was feeling extremely stressed with work and my personal life, and I inconspicuously headed upstairs so I could let my guard down. When we find ourselves in a state of sadness we tend to do everything in our power to convince ourselves that if we were gone no one would notice. I didn't expect anyone to come looking for me, and my sister-in-law, Shannon, was definitely not the person I expected to walk into the room.

For years we never got along. When Shannon married my brother, I wanted to hate her. I was fifteen years old, we just had a fire in our house, my world was a mess, and it felt like my brother was being taken from me.

Fast-forward sixteen years later. As I was sitting in the corner of the room crying Shannon walked in. She just sat there, placed her hand on me, and listened, patiently waiting for me to open up. It was a long night, but when we made our way downstairs I no longer saw her as my sister-in-law, but as my sister.

November 12

♥

Act: Go to an event to support a friend or family member.

Quote: "What you do today is the history you make tomorrow." ~Henry Ford

Reflection: True support has no strings attached. It's based less on believing in the cause or idea and more on believing in the individual. For some, discouragement is a fueling mechanism, propelling them to rise above and prove to those rooting against them that they can. But for many, discouragement is a stumbling block from which they may never recover.

Muster up an ounce of support and confidence in a family member or friend and you can help them achieve their goals. If the world was filled with more people empowering one another instead of tearing each other down, think of all the great inventions and innovations that would be created. Let's do away with the constant need to criticize and watch how the full weight of your support can lift someone up to great heights.

November 13th

✺

Act: Take a moment to acknowledge an act of kindness someone has performed. Not only will it make the person feel good, you can be sure they will be likely to repeat it in the future.

Quote: "Do something wonderful; people may imitate it." ~Albert Schweitzer

Reflection: Acknowledging the common courtesy shown by another not only increases your awareness to spot opportunities for kindness more frequently, it also inspires, empowers, and motivates the do-gooder to continuously seek out moments to infuse kindness into the world. It's a ripple effect. Think of the lives touched, the days brightened, and the positive vibes and energy set into the world all because you took the time to notice.

November 14th

Act: Today when you see garbage on the street, instead of walking past it, throw it out. You just may inspire others to follow suit and think twice before littering.

Quote: "Do what you can, with what you have, where you are." ~Theodore Roosevelt

Reflection: It started off as just a typical Sunday afternoon at the Asbury Park beach with a mix of family and friends enjoying the warm summer sun. "How would you guys like to play a game you've never played before?" I asked excitingly. Whether it was their curiosity or the fact they had their fill of sun for the day, the response was a resounding "Yes!" I pulled out a deck of Catching Kindness cards and handed a few to each person. The directions were simple. Pass a card to someone that you see performing an act of kindness. "You've been spotted performing an act of kindness. Now it's your turn to keep your eyes peeled and pass this card along the next time you catch someone in the act."

As I handed out the cards, Tom, my soon-to-be friend, walked past us and I saw him go a few steps out of his way to pick up some trash on the boardwalk, walk over to a garbage can, and throw it away. Several yards later he did it again and yet again. My friends and I smiled at each other and I went to give him a card. He had no idea what I was giving him and why I was giving it to him, but seeing the smile on his face as he walked away and began reading the card was priceless. Who knows where that card may have landed, but I can imagine that Tom will smile every time he picks up trash from the street knowing that someone may very well be watching.

November 15th

🍎

Act: Start a clothing drive, toy drive, or food drive in your school. Gather a few friends and make it happen.

Quote: "When it is dark enough, you can see the stars."
~Charles Beard

Reflection: Tragedy can paralyze us, make us become bitter or cynical. But if channeled in the right way, tragedy can grow into a source of great strength and perseverance. For Lisa and the students of her school, claiming defeat because of life's unexpected curve balls was just not an option.

After learning about Rachel's Challenge, Lisa's school decided it was time for positive action. Rachel Scott was among the victims of the Columbine shooting, but her legacy, her story, and her spirit inspired a generation of children and adults to take a stand for good.

"We dedicated our school year to several community service projects that culminated with our annual Field Day. The theme: 'It's Not About Us, It's About Others,'" Lisa recalls. From collecting food for local food pantries, to contributing money to healthcare organizations for the underprivileged, to donating books for their county library, to distributing clothes to the needy—the response from the community was astounding and sparked a trend of community service projects in Lisa's school that continues until this very day.

November 16th

🌐

Act: Bring flowers to a hospital to give to patients who may not get any visitors. (Just ask a nurse who's in need of a visit.)

Quote: "A bit of fragrance always clings to the hand that gives roses." ~Robin S. Sharma

Reflection: On each Act of Kindness card was a kindness task with simple instructions, "Perform the act and pass the card to someone else to keep the kindness going." It was my dream to see those cards spread far and wide and touch people's lives. As I read through my emails one day, I was pleasantly surprised to see an email from someone named Kate in Massachusetts.

As Kate was shopping in a local mall, a random stranger had handed her an Act of Kindness card that said, "Bring flowers to a hospital to give to patients who may not get any visitors." She took the card, placed it in her pocket, and a seed of kindness was planted in Kate's mind. Later that week Kate found herself at a hospital excited and a little anxious to complete her kindness mission. She was a bit unsure if she was up for the task, but she handed the flowers she bought over to a patient named Lenore who beamed with happiness. "It felt wonderful! I wish I had thought of it before and hope to make this a monthly commitment. Thank you for brightening both my day and Lenore's."

As I read Kate's email I thought of all the joy this one card had brought. From the mysterious stranger who handed Kate the card, to Kate, to Lenore, and, of course, right back to me. And so the boomerang of kindness will continue.

November 17th

Act: Pay for the coffee of the person behind you at the drive-through.

Quote: "Always believe something wonderful is about to happen." ~Sukhraj S. Dhillon

Reflection: I've always said that the best form of kindness is when it finds you in an unexpected place and you can't seem to pinpoint its cause. Sure—life would've gone on with or without that anonymous cup of coffee. But then again, it's not the coffee that will be remembered; it's the knowledge that goodness exists. For one person it's a mere gesture of kindness, for another it may be the gesture of hope they were so desperately seeking.

November 18th

❧

Act: Buy some fast-food certificates and have them handy to gift to those in need of a warm meal.

Quote: "Remember that the happiest people are not those getting more, but those giving more." ~H. Jackson Brown, Jr.

Reflection: Being prepared for great opportunities is like buying a welcome mat; visitors suddenly start showing up at your door. If we don't prepare ourselves mentally for the greatness we can bring into the world, the opportunity may never present itself.

Imagine if we all sought kindness as we sought treasure; with our eyes peeled, our arms open and ready to receive.

November 19th

❁

Act: Treat a coworker to lunch. We can get so wrapped up in work mode that we forget to truly connect with people. Infusing the workplace with a bit of kindness can do wonders to the way we feel.

Quote: "The only way to have a friend is to be one." ~Ralph Waldo Emerson

Reflection: It was her first week in New York when Ellie began her internship with Life Vest Inside. For a high school student from Colorado to make the journey to New York and give of her time to help a cause was pretty cool in my book. Her internship began the exact week I planned to take a step back from work and focus on my writing. To say that I was busy was an understatement. So much to do and so little time! I have an unnamed tradition of treating new people to Bravo Pizza, especially those who've never had the privilege of tasting their amazing, mouthwatering sauce. Lack of time was not going to spoil tradition. When I returned from lunch I had a small gift for Ellie: a scrumptious "grandma" slice! Who would have thought that a small four-inch square slice could make someone feel so good? Seeing her enjoy the pizza was worth the extra time it took.

November 20th

❦

Act: Send a card to a friend or loved one who recently accomplished something that means a great deal to them.

Quote: "When you have a dream, you've got to grab it and never let go." ~Carol Burnett

Reflection: Venturing out and taking a risk to do something you love is never easy. It requires support that is often scarce. To pave your own path you have to tune out the cynical remarks that can deter you. While reaching the first milestone in your journey is always memorable, it's really the people standing by your side cheering you on that makes the memory unforgettable. Believing that someone can achieve his or her dream, even if it's something you perhaps deem to be impossible, is the first and essential step to ensuring it won't remain a dream for long.

November 21st

✦

Act: Be kind to your body. Go for a walk, eat a healthy salad, and load up on fruits and veggies, or take a nap if your body is calling for rest.

Quote: "The pain you feel today will be the strength you feel tomorrow." ~Ritu Ghatourey

Reflection: As life undoubtedly gets busier and busier with each passing day and the fear of potentially missing an opportunity looms over us, we tend to justify not taking the appropriate time to care for ourselves. And so we foolishly neglect to care for the most valuable vessel we've been gifted—our body, our health. What we must realize is that whether we hide behind the guise of business, family, or even acts of true altruism, a person who can't segment a few moments of kindness for themselves will ultimately come to neglect the things on their to-do list due to illness or being run-down. Let's show the necessary appreciation for our body and our health, both of which have a big hand in all the accomplishments we pride ourselves on. Taking the time to care for your well-being isn't selfish. The stronger you are mind, body, and soul, the greater energy you will be able to give forward to the world.

November 22nd

Act: Nominate someone for an award or honor. Simply head online and you'll be amazed at the countless opportunities that exist with a click of a button.

Quote: "The most important thing is to try and inspire people so that they can be great in whatever they want to do." ~Kobe Bryant

Reflection: It's the extraordinary acts of ordinary individuals that inspire people. It instills in us the belief that we need not be anything more than ourselves to have a positive impact on the world.

One random day my friend Robert surprised me with a trip to Madison Square Garden to meet the Knicks players before the game. As a kid who grew up playing basketball, this was a huge deal for me. On that day I would get the opportunity to be on the court where it all goes down.

Halftime came and I was unexpectedly called to center court to join John Starks, a childhood icon, to accept the Sweetwater Clifton Memorial Award for community service. I was overwhelmed with feelings of joy and humility knowing that I was accepting the award on behalf of all those who believed just as strongly as I did that building a kinder world is possible.

I later found out that Robert himself had nominated me for the award. His kindness won that day.

November 23rd

Act: Help your parent or roommate prepare the Thanksgiving table for dinner. Quality time; plus, give the table an extra special touch of you.

Quote: "Many hands make light work." ~John Heywood

Reflection: Very often it's not the grand gestures of kindness but the small hints that embody what kindness truly means. An extra touch of care and an eye for detail can transform an ordinary table into an elegant dining experience, making all those present feel special. Colored napkins, a bouquet of flowers, an interesting tablecloth, place settings, or something as simple as the way you fold the napkins can do just the trick.

November 24th

♥

Act: Make a list of everything you love about your best friend and give it to him or her to read and preserve forever.

Quote: "Things spoken can be forgotten and forgiven, but the written word has the power to change the course of history, to alter our lives." ~Teresa Mummert

Reflection: It's those who are closest to us that need to hear our appreciation the most.

Years had passed, but one of my former students still kept a letter I'd written him when he was my student. He told me that he continued to open it year after year any time he started to lose hope. I couldn't believe that a few moments I spent years ago would give him reason to continue pushing forward years later.

November 25th

◉

Act: Make eye contact and say "thank you" to everyone you encounter today who provides a service or makes your life easier even in the slightest way.

Quote: "If the only prayer you ever say in your entire life is 'thank you,' it will be enough." ~Meister Eckhart

Reflection: Years ago a friend of mine ran out of gas on the side of the highway. Before he had a chance to call for help a stranger pulled over to find out if everything was okay. Upon hearing the situation he sped off in search of gas without hesitation. He came back with an extra can of gas, poured a bit into the tank, and drove off almost immediately. My friend barely had the opportunity to thank him and was taken aback by his kindness and lack of need for validation.

The stranger had lent a helping hand without need of validation, reminding my friend to keep his eyes peeled for those in need down the road.

November 26th

🍂

Act: Come across a stray animal? Take some time to bring it to the animal shelter or simply make a phone call. Your call may help reunite an owner with his or her pet.

Quote: "The worst sin toward our fellow creatures is not to hate them, but to be indifferent to them: that's the essence of inhumanity." ~George Bernard Shaw

Reflection: Kindness isn't simply the way we respond when the world is looking at us. Kindness is found in the whispers, the undetectable acts of compassion and love, and the recognition that we are all here to see each other through.

November 27th

🍎

Act: Volunteer to be a tutor or mentor in school, especially if there is an area in which you excel and can help another student.

Quote: "Experience is not what happens to you; it is what you do with what happens to you." ~Aldous Huxley

Reflection: I was extremely shy as an adolescent. After going through a severe depression in tenth grade and spending the next year and a half getting to know myself, I finally found my voice. During a high school seminar discussion on the topic of hardships, I found the courage to raise my hand and contribute to the conversation, drawing on my past experiences. To my surprise, my peers, who I had been intimidated by in the past, found comfort in my words. It was then that I discovered the transformative power of giving to another and as I continued to give, the scars began to fade. What I found was that the more I gave, the more I healed. With the most natural ease, I stepped into the role of mentor, focusing on kids, such as myself, who simply needed help to begin to see themselves.

Act: Make a donation to your favorite charity or cause. Maybe even set aside a percentage of your income if you're capable.

Quote: "Next time you talk to a charity, don't ask them about the level of their overhead, ask them about the scale of their dreams." ~Dan Pallotta

Reflection: Giving fuels me. I wanted to find a way to remind myself that any money I made was given to me to help others and so I set aside 10 percent of every dollar I earned to give to charity.

The simple action of taking from our pocket to give to another unleashed a tremendous amount of reward and blessing. It's an acknowledgment that we are here to help see each other through, that we are all connected, that one man's gain is a gain for humanity as a whole.

When I started Life Vest Inside and stopped drawing a salary, the happiness from giving 10 percent of my earnings was gone and so four years into working on Life Vest Inside I was excited to give a $10,000 check to the Pay it Forward Foundation. In a world where competition is often the name of the game, I felt privileged to genuinely collaborate with a nonprofit of similar values to my own organization.

As fate would have it, less than twenty-four hours after writing that check, Life Vest Inside won a voting contest and was awarded a $10,000 grant on Giving Tuesday. Kindness always finds its way back.

November 29th

Act: Give an extra tip to your local barista or server today.

Quote: "Sometimes when we are generous in small, barely detectable ways, it can change someone else's life forever." ~Margaret Cho

Reflection: A little gratitude on your part can improve the countless encounters customers will undoubtedly have as they're served with an extra bit of energy and positivity on that very day.

November 30th

Act: Grab a doggy bag after a big dinner out and give it to the first person you see who could use a nutritious meal.

Quote: "Kindness is the golden chain by which society is bound together." ~Johann Wolfgang von Goethe

Guest Reflection: I got a quick bite with my friend Shane one night, and as we chatted, Shane noticed that a couple left, leaving behind a half plate of food each. Shane asked the waiter to box up the leftover food in hopes of finding someone in need. A few hours later, I received a text from Shane informing me that the leftover food found its rightful owner. It was shared with a mother and daughter who had not eaten all day.

The simple idea that no food should be wasted led to a meal for two unsuspecting strangers. ~Jeff Kuske

December 1st

❀

Act: Surprise your coworkers on a Monday morning with some breakfast treats!

Quote: "I want to be the kind of person that kind people like and want to be like." ~Jarod Kintz

Reflection: When he walked into the office Monday morning, one of the newest interns had brought in a platter of breakfast pastries. He had no idea that the past weekend was a rather challenging one for me. Waking up that morning was harder than most days and I was uneasy about the week to come. It was his first week as an intern but it was clear that working at an organization that embodies kindness was exactly where he was meant to be. His unexpected surprise shed my Monday blues almost instantly.

December 2nd

✄

Act: Find a public wish list online and send a gift to a stranger.

Quote: "There are no strangers here; only friends you haven't yet met." ~William Butler Yeats

Reflection: When we count down the days to momentous occasions like birthdays, anniversaries, holidays, and graduations, we're generally filled with a sense of excitement and anticipation. It's more than the thrill of receiving a gift; it's the knowledge that on that day it's your moment to be surrounded by people who love you.

Giving when it's least expected brings with it an even greater thrill, an extra dose of excitement.

With no sense of obligation on either end, there is a subtle beauty. Serving as a reminder that even on the days you may not be publicly celebrated, someone out there is celebrating the fact that you exist.

December 3rd

✦

Act: On your day off, take the time to kick-start your morning with a nutritious breakfast. You deserve a little pampering. There's a reason they call it the most important meal of the day.

Quote: "If you are losing your leisure, look out! You may be losing your soul." ~Logan Pearsall Smith

Reflection: To feel good on the outside, you need to care for what's on the inside. By paying attention to our well-being and indulging from time to time, we free our minds. So head to the kitchen for a hearty breakfast and remember that the higher the quality of gas we fill ourselves with, the further distance we will travel.

December 4th

Act: List five positive character traits you possess. Think of small, tangible ways you take them to the next level.

Quote: "Accept no one's definition of your life; define yourself." ~Harvey Fierstein

Reflection: Spotting strengths within our weaknesses is always a challenge. We're so quick to judge ourselves, criticize our flaws, and downplay our accomplishments. "You're your own worst enemy," my mom used to tell me. I learned long ago that you can't give in to other's judgments or, even more likely, your own.

December 5th

Act: Send a small gift, write a handwritten note, or make a call to a family member you've been out of touch with or fighting with. It's not always about who's right or wrong.

Quote: "Be patient and understanding. Life is too short to be vengeful or malicious." ~Phillips Brooks

Reflection: A woman recently approached me after a talk I had given. She'd received an Act of Kindness card that read, "Make up with a friend; fighting isn't worth it." She had been fighting with her aunt and went into detail about the argument and how hurt she's been by it all. She felt she received this card for a very specific reason. "Orly, how do I do this act? I know it's important and it truly kills me inside, but how do you begin to forgive?" She began to cry.

There's no magic recipe I could tell her to truly get to the heart of that question. But I did share a tip. Don't go on the attack. Understand that people are genuinely and inherently good. Often we don't expect our actions to cause so much pain. However, once we attack someone we give them no choice but to defend and counterattack. Acknowledge the good that person has done for you, let them know that you recognize they would never intentionally harm you, and calmly explain how their actions made you feel. By altering the way we communicate and becoming more sensitive to how another person is hearing the conversation, the end result will be far more positive.

December 6th

♥

Act: Go through your closet and wear something that a loved one bought you. (Even the funny-looking holiday sweater from Grandma!) Send them a picture with the words "Thank you!"

Quote: "I've learned that you shouldn't go through life with a catcher's mitt on both hands. You need to be able to throw something back." ~Maya Angelou

Reflection: In giving gratitude we awaken the emotions of compassion, empathy, love, and kindness—all of which are cornerstones to a life filled with happiness.

December 7th

Act: Use your indoor voice.

Quote: "The more tranquil a man becomes, the greater is his success, his influence, his power for good. Calmness of mind is one of the beautiful jewels of wisdom." ~James Allen

Reflection: Out to dinner with friends or family? Getting together can be extremely exciting, and the enthusiasm and energy can hit record levels. Be sure to show respect for those dining around you by using your indoor voice. Let's start making our choices with a kindness mindset in place.

December 8th

Act: Bring reusable bags with you to the grocery store.

Quote: "The measure of who we are is what we do with what we have." ~Vince Lombardi

Reflection: Sometimes the little things are the big things. Isn't it wonderful that a simple positive action has the potential to become something impactful? You matter because your actions matter regardless of how trivial they seem sometimes. Own it and soon you'll see just how big the small things are.

December 9th

🍎

Act: Send a letter of appreciation to your child's teacher or one of your former teachers.

Quote: "A teacher affects eternity; he can never tell where his influence stops." ~Henry Adams

Reflection: The seven years I taught middle school were the most transformative of my life. With a smile on my face I would pop out of bed ready and excited to instill a bit of knowledge into young minds thirsty to grow. Not just mere facts and figures, but knowledge of life, of the world still awaiting them, of dreams still not dreamt, of potential still undiscovered.

Teachers love and care for their students in more ways than you know. A small reminder on your part that they are making a difference will help them to keep on making that difference.

December 10th

Act: Donate old textbooks.

Quote: "An investment in knowledge pays the best interest."
~Benjamin Franklin

Reflection: Education is the pathway to tolerance. Share your knowledge and resources proudly.

December 11th

Act: Offer to share your umbrella on a rainy day.

Quote: "Do your little bit of good where you are; it's those little bits of good put together that overwhelm the world."
~Desmond Tutu

Reflection: He could have walked by and pretended not to notice. But on that very rainy day, when I approached an unsuspecting stranger asking for some protection from the rain as I walked to my car a half a block down the road, he took the extra minute to engage without fear or hesitation. His kindness still lingers in my subconscious every time I find myself walking in the rain. I now look at rainy days as an opportunity to offer someone else my umbrella and pass on the favor.

December 12th

Act: Treat a stranger to a pizza. Perhaps enjoy it together.

Quote: "The most exquisite pleasure is giving pleasure to others." ~Jean de La Bruyère

Reflection: As I sat down to eat my pizza and relax for a few minutes amid my chaotic day, I saw a man standing patiently waiting for a seat to open up. "Would you like to sit down? I don't mind." He thanked me, smiled, and sat down. We conversed for a bit, asking some of the typical first-meeting questions. I excused myself to get another slice and when I came back he was finishing up. He wished me luck with my non-profit and I wished him luck with his business. I stopped by the cashier on the way out to pay for my meal, only to find out that it had been covered. I never saw that man again, but I won't forget that meal or his kindness.

December 13th

✿

Act: Open your eyes! There is something unique and special within each person you meet, from the president of the company to the mail attendant. See the beauty beyond the titles.

Quote: "There is nothing so rewarding as to make people realize that they are worthwhile in this world." ~Bob Anderson

Reflection: I was directing the school play and would spend long nights at rehearsals. After the students left the auditorium, I would stay behind to work on the set, props, and other odds and ends. Every night Wilfred, the school janitor, would walk in, broom and shovel in hand, to clean the remnants of all the things the students left behind. He kept to himself, but had a kindness in his eyes that made me introduce myself. "I'm Orly! What's your name?"

From that day forward Wilfred and I have greeted each other with a big smile and a warm hello.

December 14th

Ⓜ️

Act: Out for dinner? Pull out the chair for your guest. Date or not, it simply shows a bit of extra thought and concern.

Quote: "Act as if what you do makes a difference. It does."
~William James

Reflection: Some view it as chivalry, others see it as simple manners. I see it as a way of saying "welcome." It may be a lost gesture from the past, but it can make the recipient not only feel respected, but appreciated as well. So have a seat, I'm glad you're here.

December 15th

⭐

Act: Treat yourself to an extra-long hot shower or bubble bath. Enjoy that slice of cake that you pass by every day. Splurge on an item you have been saving up for.

Quote: "You are worth more than the value you have placed on yourself." ~The Amity Affliction

Reflection: Life passes in the blink of an eye. So revel in the wonderful things it has to offer. And remember, giving to ourselves opens us up to give back to others in an even greater way. "You are worth it." Repeat those words to yourself over and over again and soon enough you'll begin to believe it, live it, and own it.

December 16th

Act: Next time you're faced with the choice to purchase an item that may have been stolen or pirated, overcome your inclination. No one will know the internal struggle you faced, but you will, and you'll have grown because of it.

Quote: "It is not hard to make decisions when you know what your values are." ~Roy Disney

Reflection: When I stumbled on the singer Julia Westlin's YouTube channel, my heart was moved and her voice spoke to me. I could have easily downloaded the music from her channel and listened to my heart's content, or I could ensure that Julia continues on her musical pursuit so that years from now a whole new slew of people may get inspired by her beautiful voice. Money was tight, but I wanted to contribute even if in a small way to show that her work and her art matters. Ever since, I've been supporting her on Patreon, a platform that allows you to contribute each time a creator puts out a new video or song. For $5 a month I got the unique opportunity to become a part of the process and know that not only have I taken, but I've given back.

December 17th

🏠

Act: While tucking your children in bed tonight, spend a few extra minutes to tell them that you love them and, more important, point out something that makes them unique and wonderful.

Quote: "Always kiss your children goodnight—even if they're already asleep." ~H. Jackson Brown, Jr.

Reflection: "You're not like everyone else; you're special!" My dad would whisper these words to me each night as he tucked me into bed. It made me feel like there was something great waiting for me to accomplish. It's that certainty that set me on the path I'm still on today. Having someone see the beauty within me allowed me to begin to see it within myself. Our children are our legacy and our words and actions are the seeds to build a foundation for them to grow and spread their roots.

December 18th

♥

Act: Plan a spa day for you and your spouse, partner, or friend.

Quote: "We don't remember days . . . we remember moments."
~Cesare Pavese

Reflection: We all deserve a bit of pampering every once in a while. What better way to spend it than enjoying each other's company in a relaxed atmosphere?

The benefits of investing in our relationships are found in the happiness we feel when heading to bed at the end of a long day, the satisfaction of knowing you have someone to lean on, and the safety we feel when sharing a simple moment. Like anything else in life, the more you give to it the more it will give back.

December 19th

Act: In-box reaching record highs? Resolve to get to zero.

Quote: "Nobody made a greater mistake than he who did nothing because he could only do a little." ~Edmund Burke

Reflection: Writing a book was unchartered territory for me. How would I segment time to write and also be mindful of responding to people in a timely manner for work? Fearful of the overwhelming emails I would be left to tackle after writing the book, I resolved to allocate an hour in the early morning and the late evening to get back to as many people as possible.

For that hour, the people who had reached out to me were the only thing on my mind. Many people called me foolish, saying "Put your away message on"; "Leave them for a later date"; "No one actually responds to all their emails." I couldn't do it; it wasn't in my nature. An unlikely email from a fan of Life Vest Inside reaching out to share their feelings of despair and hopelessness was all the proof I needed that those hours were the most important times of my day. I don't know what would have happened had I not been there to respond, but I can tell you that a beautiful friendship emerged because I was there. "I can't believe you took the time to answer me." That response always shocks me. The way I see it is how could I not respond? "You saved my life," he said. I don't know if I actually saved his life, but he brought a great deal more meaning into mine.

December 20th

❖

Act: Take a shorter shower today or start becoming more mindful of how long you let the water run while brushing your teeth.

Quote: "We never know the worth of water till the well is dry."
~Thomas Fuller

Reflection: When my cousin from Israel spent the summer in my house, I learned such a powerful lesson one morning while brushing my teeth next to her in a shared bathroom. I let the water run as I washed up, but I noticed that she barely used any water, being mindful to open the faucet only in the fractions of a second when she needed it. It seemed strange to me, but living in Israel, a country in which water was sparse, created a mindfulness that followed her on her travels around the world. An understanding that even the simple things we do behind closed doors impact the lives of others. It may seem straightforward, but changing our routine is never easy. A small shift on our part can lead to a great shift for the world. Brushing my teeth was never the same.

December 21st

🍎

Act: Visit your old school and pop in on a former teacher that impacted your life. Let them know how they've positively influenced you for the better and remind them how awesome they are.

Quote: "Feeling gratitude, and not expressing it, is like wrapping a present and not giving it." ~William Arthur Ward

Reflection: My most prized possession isn't money stashed away, a contact list of well-connected people within my network, or a contract of my greatest business deal of all time. It's five binders filled with pages upon pages of letters of appreciation from hundreds of students I've had the pleasure of knowing throughout my seven years of teaching. As I flip through the pages a common phrase repeats itself time and time again: "You've changed my life!" My eyes fill with tears no matter how many times I read this. The power of gratitude and acknowledgment are never-ending. The years may pass, the ink on the paper fades, but the experience stays with me.

December 22nd

Act: Stop by your local police or fire department to drop off some deliciously baked homemade cookies. Thank them for all the work they do for your community.

Quote: "Only a life lived for others is a life worthwhile." ~Albert Einstein

Reflection: Day in and day out they risk their lives to ensure our safety. Before the opportunity to express gratitude passes, let us take a moment to acknowledge the service of those who are in constant pursuit of our well-being. It may not always be newsworthy, but it's the simple acts of heroism and bravery that sometimes need to be commended the most. It doesn't require a large gesture, but can simply be a heartfelt "thank you."

December 23rd

Act: Out running errands? Ring a couple of friends or family members to ask if they need something while you're out.

Quote: "No one is useless in this world who lightens the burdens of another." ~Charles Dickens

Reflection: "I'm thinking of you." When these words are uttered mindlessly time and time again, they can lose meaning for the person hearing them. I think you'll find that a small gesture can elevate those same words to more than sounds and syllables, helping a person see just how special you think they are.

December 24th

Act: Create a kindness kit: Fill a bag with socks, a blanket, mouthwash, gloves, a snack, and anything else you can think of. Keep it in your trunk ready to give to someone in need this holiday season.

Quote: "Kindness in words creates confidence. Kindness in thinking creates profoundness. Kindness in giving creates love." ~Lao Tzu

Reflection: For most, socks aren't an extravagant gift, but for those who are homeless it can make a big difference.

Having suffered from homelessness in the past, my friend Jeff felt a continued desire to serve those in need. Jeff set out to a homeless shelter with dozens of socks in his arms. As he approached the shelter, he saw a homeless woman sitting on the curb and offered her a pair. "I don't have any money," she responded. He explained that it was a gift with no strings attached. Word spread, and before he knew it sixty pairs of socks were given out in less than ten minutes.

December 25th

Act: Send a letter of appreciation to someone who has made your life memorable and meaningful. Knowing that we are appreciated propels us to give forward even greater. What better time to show gratitude than on this special day.

Quote: "The only people with whom you should try to get even with are those who have helped you." ~John E. Southard

Reflection: If you ever doubted the power of a letter, think back to a time when you were the recipient. We all need to remind one another that we are loved and appreciated. Today's job is to spread love and gratitude.

December 26th

❦

Act: Surprise someone with an unexpected gift.

Quote: "Carry out a random act of kindness, with no expectation of reward, safe in the knowledge that one day someone might do the same for you." ~Princess Diana

Reflection: One day there was an unexpected knock at my door. A surprise package was delivered, filled with yummy chocolate treats wrapped up inside that made my heart skip a beat and filled me with an overwhelming sense of happiness. There was an accompanying small note with two seemingly ordinary words that made it ten times better for me: "Just because . . ."

December 27th

★

Act: Doing good comes from feeling good, so treat yourself to a hot chocolate, book a massage, schedule that dance class, or take an extra ten minutes during your lunch hour. You deserve it!

Quote: "Self-love is the source of all our other loves." ~Pierre Corneille

Reflection: What is life if not the stolen moments we take for ourselves? Our very own pause button; a time to reevaluate, a time to get centered, a time to remind ourselves of the importance of our journey. If simply doing something personal for yourself can make you feel good, just think of the lives you will touch as a result of the energy you restore within yourself.

December 28th

Act: Give an anonymous donation, of any amount, to a cause you care about.

Quote: "The measure of your life will not be in what you accumulate, but what you give away." ~Dr. Wayne Dyer

Reflection: Whether you give a dollar or a thousand dollars, the simple act of giving what you can grants you the opportunity to have a hand in all the wonderful advancements the organization or individual will make in the world. Remember, you were given what you have for a purpose; put it to good use.

It's one thing to give, it's another thing to give anonymously, knowing that your intention is purely for the sake of giving. Giving publicly has a positive impact as well, inspiring others to give. However, you'll find the inner level of satisfaction is far greater when your gift is given behind the scenes.

December 29th

🏠

Act: Plan a sit-down no-tech roommate night.

Quote: "Most of us spend too much on what is urgent and not enough time on what is important." ~Stephen Covey

Reflection: For some households it may be a given but for many others, designating a tech-free night seems impossible. Buy a couple of board games, bake some desserts, and you never know—this may just become the backbone of keeping you and your roommates grounded and united. I can only say that for me, tech-free Friday nights are the thing I count down to every week. The world may be hectic but in our home there is an amazing sense of calm for that one night a week. Some of my greatest laughs, most heartfelt talks, and happiest memories were created on those "non-tech" Friday nights.

December 30th

♥

Act: Open your heart and tell someone, "I love you." It may be scary to say, but it's worth putting your heart on the line.

Quote: "The course of true love never did run smooth." ~William Shakespeare

Reflection: The ability to let our guard down and remove the masks we use to protect ourselves takes great strength. Vulnerability is letting someone into the recesses of your soul and risking that they may end up letting you down. While being vulnerable may be scary, the benefits and potential victory that it can bring are more than worth it. It's no wonder Alfred Lord Tennyson so eloquently wrote, "'Tis better to have loved and lost than never to have loved at all."

December 31st

◉

Act: In a fight? Had a disagreement? Time to make things right and bring clarity before starting the new year.

Quote: "You can't always sit in your corner of the forest and wait for people to come to you. You have to go to them sometimes." ~Winnie the Pooh

Reflection: Disagreements are rooted in misunderstanding and lack of communication. When the rage begins to set in, there are two choices; react, or take a moment to process it all so that the next step you take will be one that leads you to a place of clarity. There are over seven billion people in the world, each with their own way of perceiving the world and the people around them; disagreements are inevitable, but how we choose to react is exactly that: a choice. Confrontation forces us to become vulnerable and let our guard down. Make the resolve to do it and do it with mindful sensitivity. You're bound to feel a huge weight lifted and a friendship saved. What better way to end the year than with peace of mind, heart, and soul.

Acknowledgments

Writing a book is never a one-person journey. There are those who act as a constant beacon of support and encouragement at the times when you're ready to throw in the towel and question if you'll ever get through. Then there are those who join you in the trenches, doing the tedious legwork to remove some of the burden, allowing you to focus on the bigger picture. And then there are those who don't even know that they've significantly impacted your journey. They live your message of kindness and unknowingly teach you bits and pieces about life in their own special way. By doing so, their essence becomes a part of your voice, your inner strength, how you see the world, the person you've become and continue to strive to be.

I'm fortunate to have had all three groups join me on this exciting journey of writing my very first book.

To my Grampsi, my captain. You may no longer physically be with us, but looking at your picture on my desk day in and day out during the writing process and knowing that this book would be dedicated to your memory is what pushed me through. You didn't simply "do" kindness, you lived it through and through and by so doing have had a great impact on me. To Nana, you have been such a great source of strength and love.

To my mom and dad, my family, my everything, thank you for challenging me through it all. While we may not always see eye to eye, making you proud of me has pushed me to strive be the best person I can be.

To my students, while I left my teaching position

2011, my seven years teaching all of you was the greatest gift anyone could receive and has truly been the most transformative of my life. You all made me strive to become the best version of myself and each of you, in your own unique way, has left an imprint on my heart that will last a lifetime.

To the Life Vest Inside Kindness Ambassadors, Group Leaders, staff, interns, and fans who strengthen me every day with words of encouragement and empowerment, seeing me through the hurdles that many would say are insurmountable. It is your belief in me and the mission of kindness that inspire me to continue giving with my whole heart without question. Naming everyone that has impacted me on this journey would fill a book of its own, but I would like to make special mention of a few who have joined me the in trenches: Louis Meli (my angel of kindness), Jewel Fries, Lagunesvary Ganesan, Afrah Farahid, Phaneendra Jonnalagadda, Gary Salvit, David Beltran, Shelby Robinson, Terese Rolke, Birgit Nisu, Alexa Christodoulou, Jennifer Mortensen, Afrah Farahid, Zilma Hamouche, and hundreds more who submitted their stories of kindness. I wish I could list you all by name.

To Jeff Kuske (AKA Mayor Jeff), you're not only a Kindness Ambassador, you've become a great friend and have stuck by my side day in and day out as I wrote the book. Reviewing entries, pushing me to meet my deadlines and never losing faith for a single moment. Hardships have most certainly arisen, but I will be forever grateful to you for being my accountability partner until the very end.

To Justin Taylor, someone I like to call my angel. Your support has been unparalleled; without it Life Vest Inside would simply not be. Your humility, your willingness to give wholeheartedly, and the anonymous surprise packages you have sent me over the years have fueled me forward and kept me going. When I think of you, all I can do is smile.

To Lydia Criss Mays, a woman who has been there from the very start, a woman who has inspired me to See Beautiful in myself and all that surrounds me. Thank you for your support, your loving kindness, and the inspiration you so genuinely infuse into my heart and the hearts of all those you meet. You are a true kindness hero.

Tracing the history of how this book came to be, I would have never had this wonderful opportunity without being given a chance to speak at TED back in 2013. After hearing me speak, Amanda Slavin, CEO of Catalyst Creative, reached out to both me and her dear friend Tony Hsieh about inviting me to speak at Catalyst Creative in Downtown Vegas. The collisions that came about from that unforgettable week amaze me until this very day. It was there that I had the fortune to meet Will Schwalbe, EVP at Macmillan, and the seed for this book was planted. Thank you, Will, for taking a chance on me and seeing something in me before I even saw it in myself.

To the amazing team at Macmillan. From Bryn Clark for ensuring the book would be the best book it can be, to Julianne Lewis, my speaking agent, and of course Lisa Queen, my literary agent.

To all of the authors who inspire me through their writing, through their heart, and through their soul. Catherine Ryan Hyde, Brad Meltzer, Roger Nierenberg, R. J. Palacio, Mark Victor Hansen, Rhonda Byrne, and so many more. Just a reminder that your work matters!

Finally, there is ONE that stands above the rest. To Hashem*, the one who has been by my side through it all, the good times, the bad times, and all the times in between. To Hashem, who has seen me at my best, seen me at my worst, yet through it all accepts me for who I am and in seemingly undetectable ways

* *Hashem is another term for G-d*

has encouraged me and empowered me to strive for more. It's no secret that faith has been my guiding light since childhood. To be honest, without faith I wouldn't be the person I am today and, while the people in my life play a big role in the person I've become, I would have never made it through the storms of life without Hashem as my north star.